THE DEVELOPMENT OF
SOCIAL SKILLS
BY BLIND AND VISUALLY IMPAIRED STUDENTS

Exploratory Studies and Strategies

Compiled and edited by Sharon Zell Sacks
with Linda S. Kekelis
and Robert J. Gaylord-Ross

American Foundation for the Blind
New York

*The Development of Social Skills by Blind and Visually Impaired Students:
Exploratory Studies and Strategies*
is copyright © 1992 by
American Foundation for the Blind
15 West 16th Street, New York, NY 10011

96   95   94   93   92   5 4 3 2 1

Printed in the United States of America

Library of Congress Cataloging-in-Publication Data

The development of social skills by blind and visually impaired
    students: exploratory studies and strategies/compiled and edited
    by Sharon Zell Sacks with Linda S. Kekelis and Robert J. Gaylord-Ross.
        p.   cm.
    Includes bibliographical references (p.).
    ISBN 0-89128-217-3
    1. Children, Blind—Education—United States. 2. Visually
    handicapped children—Education—United States. 3. Social skills—
    Study and teaching—United States. 4. Social intelligence—Study
    and teaching—United States.   I. Sacks, Sharon. II. Kekelis,
    Linda. III. Gaylord-Ross, Robert
    HV1664. S63D48 1992   92-18638
    371, 91'1—dc20   CIP

Photo credits: Thomas Savarino.

Chapter 10 is reprinted from the *Journal of Visual Impairment & Blindness, 80*(6), 794-797.

The study on which Chapter 4 is based and from which the guidelines in Chapter 7 were developed was supported by Social and Behavioral Sciences Research Grant #12-179 from the March of Dimes Birth Defects Foundation. The study on which Chapter 5 is based was supported by the Ross C. Purse Doctoral Scholarship from the Canadian Institute for the Blind, the Florence S. Dunlop Memorial Scholarship Fund, and the Thesis Incentive Award from the American Foundation for the Blind.

To our children:
Loren, Rebecca, Kyle, Alexa, and Asher.

Contents

PART 3: STRATEGIES FOR EDUCATORS AND IMPLICATIONS FOR FURTHER RESEARCH

Foreword

Success in employment and social activities often depends on the impression we make on other people. Aspects of personal appearance such as facial expressions and eye contact and a quick responsiveness to others are just some facets of social interaction that may be affected by the ability to see and that influence what people think of us. By observing social interactions every day, children develop at an early age many of the skills that help them to become accomplished social beings. Because so much of what we call social skills is picked up by children incidentally through watching others, blind and visually impaired children who cannot observe social interactions directly often have difficulty becoming socially adept.

Although educational efforts have focused on the academic needs of children who are blind or visually impaired, the equally vital social needs of these children have not usually received equal attention. This can often be the case in mainstream settings, where classroom teachers may be unaccustomed to the unique needs of visually impaired children and where resource-room or itinerant teachers must often spend the limited time they have in teaching adaptive skills for academic performance. Without a foundation of solid techniques for social interactions developed in their school years, visually impaired adults frequently lack the underpinnings for success in their work and personal lives.

The purpose of *The Development of Social Skills by Blind and Visually Impaired Students* is, therefore, to help researchers and practitioners understand why children who are blind or visually impaired often fail to have positive social interactions and to point the way toward intervention strategies. The book outlines the theoretical background of social-skills development, presents case studies that show the factors influencing social encounters, and suggests guidelines for helping children shape those encounters into satisfying ones. In doing so, it uses an ethnographic approach—the first time that we know of that this approach has been used in the blindness field—in which the research issues were not imposed on the data but emerged from the observations. Observational techniques that classroom teachers can use themselves with individual children have in effect been demonstrated for their use.

The findings presented here leave little doubt that the teaching of social skills needs to become recognized as an integral part of the curriculum for visually impaired students. We at the American Foundation for the Blind believe that this book will play a key role in promoting an awareness of this need. We also hope that *The Development of Social Skills* acts as a springboard for continued research and practical support for visually impaired children in this critical area of learning.

Carl R. Augusto
President and Executive Director
American Foundation for the Blind

Preface

We educators have acknowledged for years that it is desirable for most and necessary for many visually impaired children to learn social skills. Although we can identify this need intellectually, we do not seem to be able to implement a creative, sequential curriculum in this area. Part of our problem is that we have been so intent on mainstreaming that we did not acknowledge the need to stress the development of social skills. Had we done so, our efforts to integrate visually impaired children in public schools might have been much more successful. Instead, we handled the learning of social skills on a casual basis, correcting inappropriate social behavior as it occurred and, unfortunately, only when we observed it.

It is ironic that our early commitment to the integration of visually impaired children was based primarily on social needs. In the 1950s and 1960s, most schools for blind and visually impaired children still had strong academic programs, so our reason for supporting the enrollment of visually impaired children in public day schools was not based on the need to provide a stronger academic program. Rather, we stressed integration because we knew that there are significant social advantages to having visually impaired children live at home with their families, attend neighborhood schools, make friends in school and their neighborhoods, and begin to connect with their communities.

Although since its inception our profession has recognized the role of vision in learning, sighted professionals have tended to overlook the obvious in the development of social skills: Almost all the skills that we sighted people use in everyday social interactions with others have been learned by us through visual observation. We learn to use different social skills with different people, in different settings, and with different groups. We are not only socially adept, we are socially versatile. We therefore need to provide the answers to a number of issues raised when children cannot learn about social interaction by means of visual observation:

Can social-skills training be treated as "incidental" learning? Without the help of visual observation, how can visually impaired children learn to be socially adept and versatile? Will they become so simply through exposure to sighted peers? Or must someone teach them? Is it parents' or teachers' responsibility to teach social skills? Are mainstreamed visually impaired children at great risk of experiencing social isolation? And to what extent is the continuing tragic rate of unemployment among adult blind and visually impaired persons the result of their lack of social skills?

This timely and important book is one of our profession's first concerted efforts to address the need to teach social interaction skills to visually impaired children. The authors are eminently qualified to provide at least some tentative answers to our questions. Perhaps their efforts can help us address a difficult but crucial area in our curriculum.

> Philip H. Hatlen
> *Superintendent*
> *Texas School for the Blind and Visually Impaired*

Introduction

As a resource-room and itinerant teacher, I vividly remember observing the isolation and emotional pain that many blind and visually impaired children experienced in regular public school classrooms. These students lacked the social skills to start and carry on conversations, to play games effectively, and to join and feel part of a group; were uncomfortable talking about their visual impairments; and, what was most important, tried to hide the fact that they were visually impaired. In short, they did not feel happy with themselves, have a high degree of self-esteem, or see themselves as valued and unique human beings.

For me, as for many visually impaired persons, the acquisition of competent social skills in a sighted environment is an ongoing process; these skills are not easily learned and must be continuously fine-tuned throughout one's life. Because the social nuances that are necessary to function in our society are dependent on visual cues and are frequently expressed through gestures rather than speech, visually impaired persons often have difficulty establishing and maintaining social relationships with sighted people, both personally and professionally.

Although numerous blind and visually impaired children and adolescents have been integrated in public school classrooms and are successful academically, both professionals and parents are deeply concerned that such children are not learning the social skills they need to interact with their sighted peers, develop positive social relationships, and be successfully employed as adults (Bishop, 1986). The majority of these students receive disability-specific training from itinerant teachers, who concentrate on helping them maintain their academic skills and are neither trained in nor competent to teach the skills that these students will need to function socially and emotionally throughout their lives. These children will continue to be at a disadvantage in regular education classrooms and to be deprived of learning essential social skills unless activities of daily living, motor and concept development, social-skills training, and career education are incorporated into their curricula (Curry & Hatlen, 1988).

In light of this situation, a few professionals have begun to develop strategies for training blind and visually impaired students in social skills on the basis of work done by researchers with other disabled groups (see, for example, Van Hasselt, Hersen, Kazdin, Simon, & Mastanuono, 1983). However, research and practice in this field are still scant. As a result of the paucity of research and my experiences as a visually impaired person and as a teacher of visually impaired students, I began with my colleagues to explore the ways in which social-skills training can be effectively incorporated into traditional educational programs for visually impaired children.

In our initial two-year study, funded by the March of Dimes Birth Defects Foundation, Linda Kekelis and I examined the social integration of visually impaired mainstreamed kindergartners and first-graders. We used an ethnographic approach, engaging in qualitative research to investigate how visually impaired children interact with their sighted classmates. Several significant findings that emerged from this study were the foundation of the guidelines we developed for teachers of visually impaired students, regular education teachers, other professionals in the field, and parents. These strategies are the bases of the studies carried out by myself and my co-editors that are reported in this book.

The book is divided into three parts and deals with theory, research, and practice. Its purpose is twofold. The first aim is to link basic theoretical constructs of social development to the unique process that blind and visually impaired children undergo to learn and maintain social skills. From these constructs, researchers and practitioners can identify and examine problems and develop strategies to enhance the lives of these children. The second aim is to present applied research and strategies that will help practitioners and parents institute successful social-skills training in schools, at home, and in the community. Because the research presented here is basic, it is hoped that readers will investigate these issues in their observations of individual children and experiment with new strategies for social-skills training. In this way, we may be able to ensure that blind and visually impaired children and youths will gain the social competence they need to achieve to their fullest throughout their formal education and into adulthood.

Finally at this point, I would like to say that this book would not have been possible without the support and assistance of many individuals whose enthusiasm, expertise, and true commitment to our project gave us the spirit to proceed and finally produce a valued contribution to our field.

First, we would like to thank our families. They gave up many precious hours with us while we carried out observations, collected data, wrote, and edited this volume.

Next, we must acknowledge Allyson Bennett and Kathleen Kanewske for their skill, accuracy, and prompt inputting of many pages of manuscript into the final format. Their secretarial efforts helped this book become a reality.

There are so many individuals who assisted us in our research projects, and each deserves our special gratitude. In order to conduct our mainstreaming study, we sought the assistance of the Blind Babies Foundation, the Castro Valley Unified School District, and the Fremont Unified School District. Our gratitude is extended to each preschool counselor; to Margaret Kidd, director of special education in Castro Valley; and to Norman Nestor, assistant director of special education in Fremont, California. We also wish to acknowledge the resource-room teachers who coordinated our efforts at each school site—Joan Bliss, Fran Bauer-Dibble, Sue Douglas, and Charleen Okamoto—as well as the classroom teachers, Ms. Chidister, Ms. Freitas, Ms. Peterson, Mr. Santini, and Ms. Silvey.

The completion of the case study of a blind child would not have been possible without the support and cooperation of a number of individuals. We are grateful to the child's parents, who shared their insights about their daughter's social world, and to Fran Bauer-Dibble and Cindy Harrington as well.

The completion of our study of peer-mediated and teacher-directed social-skills training could not have occurred without the support of the following teachers of visually impaired students: Joan Bliss, Sandra DeFries, Sue Douglas, Charleen Okamoto, and Jill Paton. We are especially grateful to the three data collectors—Jennifer Howe, Hope Levy, and Janet Macks—who spent many hours observing students in classrooms and cafeterias and on playgrounds. Also, the talents and expertise of Dr. Leonard Marascuilo in providing statistical support and guidance cannot be forgotten. He brought statistics to life and made data analysis meaningful. He will be remembered by all of us as an integral part of our research.

We extend our thanks to Sandra Adams Curry, Dr. Philip Hatlen, and Dr. Diane Wormsley for their insights and advice regarding the content of this manuscript. We also wish to acknowledge all the students who participated in our research. They provided us with invaluable information and helped us to understand the social world of visually impaired children and youths.

Sharon Zell Sacks

Part 1: Theory

The process by which all children—including blind and visually impaired children—develop social skills is highly individual and influenced by their early learning experiences, support from their families, and their ability to mediate the social environment. However, as Warren (1984) noted, blind and visually impaired children may be at a disadvantage in acquiring the same level of social competence as their sighted peers because they lack the visual input that is critical to develop relationships and to move about independently and take charge of their environment. Therefore, to educate blind and visually impaired students in a consistent, effective way, practitioners must understand how "generic" theories of social development relate to their students' unique educational and social needs. Likewise, theory provides the basis for high-quality research whose long-term findings may be used to develop innovative practical strategies.

Although other disciplines have designed powerful training programs in the area of social skills, practice in our field has been somewhat of a folk art, in which training techniques and established approaches have been passed from one professional to another with little basis in theory or research. For example, social-skills interventions that were initially used with autistic and severely disabled persons were based on strict behavior constructs and empirical methodologies. Thus, strong philosophical beliefs have driven the formulation of numerous educational programs that sometimes ignore the needs of individual students. This state of affairs is reflected in such developments as the controversy over the use of braille versus the use of residual low vision by visually impaired students.

Many parents and professionals question the social benefits that blind and visually impaired children gain from being mainstreamed in regular education classrooms throughout their formal education. They have found that despite this experience, many students still lack the social savvy to make decisions independently, to maintain positive social relationships with both visually impaired and sighted peers, and to demonstrate skills that will be needed throughout their adult lives.

Both professionals and parents know that it is important to provide experiences that maximize positive social contacts for children. However, they are often unsure which approach should be taken or whether an approach has merit for a specific child. Chapters 1 and 2 that follow discuss theories of social development and general theories of peer relationships that may influence the social and emotional needs of blind and visually impaired children. Through theoretical analyses and case studies, these chapters define social skills and establish the context for understanding the design of research methods and the application of social-skills training to enhance the social competence of blind and visually impaired students and hence help them to be included in the lives of their sighted peers.

Chapter 1

The Social Development of Visually Impaired Children: A Theoretical Perspective

Sharon Zell Sacks

Public school programs to educate blind and visually impaired children have traditionally emphasized the importance of acquiring a requisite set of academic skills. The prevailing philosophy among educators of visually impaired children was, and still is to some degree, that given appropriate nurturing, educational placement, and training, blind or visually impaired children will develop in a similar fashion to and should be educated with sighted children.

This perspective, voiced as early as 1929 by Meyer, a prominent educator, dominated the educational structure and directed the course of mainstreaming practices for over 50 years. The goal of the teacher of visually impaired students was to provide equipment, materials, and specialized training (in braille reading and writing and use of the abacus and slate and stylus) to enhance the children's academic performance in the regular classroom (Hatlen, 1980). As a result, numerous visually impaired students who graduated from public schools in the late 1960s and 1970s did not acquire the social skills they needed to function independently (Bateman, 1965; Jones, Lavine, & Shell, 1972; McGuinnes, 1970).

With the passage of P.L. 94-142, the Education for All Handicapped Children Act, greater emphasis was placed on providing educational services in the least restrictive environment (Winzer, Rogow, & David, 1987). Thus, many blind and visually impaired students spent more time in regular classrooms and received fewer direct services from teachers of visually impaired students. This approach left many children socially isolated and academically limited and resulted in a "more restrictive environment" (Gresham, 1981, p. 140; see also Eagelstein, 1975; Hoben & Lindstrom, 1980). The children were neither accepted by their sighted peers nor trained in age-appropriate social skills that would foster their interaction with sighted children, which are critical for effective mainstreaming (Bishop, 1986). Without structured training for both sighted and blind and visually impaired children, simple social or physical proximity between the groups may be counterproductive (Asher & Gottman, 1981; Asher, Oden, & Gottman, 1977; Cowen, Peterson, Babigian, Izzo, & Trost, 1973; Fredericks et al., 1978; Gottlieb & Budoff, 1973; Gresham, 1982; Quintal, 1986; Sacks & Reardon, 1989).

Educators of visually impaired children acknowledge the importance of functional skills for their students. However, they are less clear about the children's unique developmental differences that stem from limited or no vision and the specific effects such limitations may have in the mainstream classroom, particularly on social development and the acquisition of social skills. Reardon and Sacks's (1985) hierarchy of nonacademic skills stresses the importance of attaining a repertoire of socially acceptable behaviors and skills to achieve greater independence and increased feelings of self-worth. Without such a grounding, higher-order skills (daily living skills, leisure skills, work skills, and academic pursuits) remain isolated components that blind and visually impaired children do not transfer to future endeavors with peers, especially in the mainstream environment.

Therefore, it is important to know which social skills are considered appropriate, to examine the applicability of theories of social development to blind and visually impaired persons, and to evaluate the importance that these theories attribute to interactions with peers. Then one can begin to develop strategies to effect positive changes in social behavior.

DEFINITIONS OF SOCIAL SKILLS

This section outlines three models for defining social skills—the trait model, the molecular or component model, and the process or systems model—and briefly evaluates their utility for blind and visually impaired children. These models were developed for work with other severely impaired populations and hence are not directly applicable to blind and visually impaired people. However, the insights gained and the inferences that can be made from them are beneficial in establishing programs in social-skills training.

The Trait Model

The trait model assumes that "skillfulness" in social behaviors is predetermined and imbedded in one's personality structure and hence that an individual's level of social behavior will remain stable and consistent over time and across settings. This model is not widely used because it has not been demonstrated empirically (McFall, 1982). If it were applied to blind or visually impaired individuals, one might assume that their passive or "antisocial" behavior is simply a part of their personality makeup and that no action could elicit any change (Van Hasselt, 1983a).

The Molecular or Component Model

According to this approach, social skills are observable units of learned verbal and nonverbal behavior that, when combined, can foster successful interactions in specific situations (Foster & Ritchey, 1979; Hersen & Bellack, 1977; McFall, 1982). As Kelly (1982, p.3) noted, "individuals use [these skills] in interpersonal situations to obtain or to maintain reinforcement from their environment."

One drawback of this model is that trainers or raters establish what is considered socially skilled behavior. Hence, there is great variability in the selection and definition of target behaviors, the means by which behaviors are observed and measured, and the overall evaluation of the acquisition of skills across settings and time (Bellack, 1983; Bellack, Hersen, & Turner, 1978).

Training strategies based on the molecular model have been used widely, especially in the fields of psychology, psychiatry, and education. Similar strategies have been employed with visually impaired children and adults on a limited basis (see Van Hasselt, 1983b, for a review of the research). This model has helped many blind and visually impaired people who have difficulty perceiving, modeling, and acknowledging the behaviors of others (Farkas, Sherick, Matson, & Loebig, 1981).

The Process Model

In the process model, it is assumed that social skills are the components of specific actions (looks or nods, for example) or sequences of behavior that create specific encounters (such as greetings) and that they are contingent upon rules (Argyle, 1980; Trower, 1982). According to Trower (1982, p. 418), "such components are learned by experience or observation, retained in memory in symbolic form, and subsequently retrieved for use in the construction of episodes." This approach promotes the utilization of goals to attain a set of socially skilled behaviors; it relies on one's ability to perceive both the physical environment and the internal needs of others. Using this model, an individual can monitor the immediate situation and evaluate his or her behavior in that situation in relation to external feedback (verbal or nonverbal) from others and an internal assessment (cognitive representative or logical thinking) (Argyle & Kendon, 1967). The components of such a model are as follows:

Perceptions of other people. The ability to respond effectively to another's needs or desires.

Taking the role of others. The ability not only to recognize another's feelings, but to understand what the other person is thinking or feeling.

Nonverbal accompaniments of speech. During an interaction, a combination of speech and nonverbal cues to acquire appropriate proximity and orientation. Such elements are highly contingent on hearing and sight.

Rewards. The ability to acknowledge and reinforce another's social behavior or initiations through a smile or head nod, for example.

Self-presentation. The ability to send cues to another person to indicate one's role, status, or identity.

Situations and their rules. The ability to obtain the full meaning of a given set of rules that structure a specific encounter, sometimes through visual feedback if the rules are intricate.

Sequences of interactions. The ability to place a series of verbal and nonverbal cues in a certain order to obtain a positive outcome.

Cognitive-behavioral interventions involving problem solving and verbal mediation have been used with children with behavior disorders (Meichenbaum, 1977) and with hyperactive children to enhance controlled behavior in anger-producing situations (Hinshaw, Henker, & Whalen, 1984).

However, the process model may have limited utility for blind and visually impaired children. The ability to monitor a social situation and to establish goals involves the integration of a visual sense along with auditory and cognitive skills. Without vision, it is difficult to perceive another's actions and feelings, and mediation and interpretation by another individual may be required. Furthermore, a person who has had limited exposure to different types of environments or individuals will have limited experiential learning, which may hamper his or her ability to integrate isolated social behaviors into a series of expanded, intricate social encounters.

Nevertheless, a problem-solving, self-monitoring process-model approach with visually impaired children, aged 8–10, in mainstream settings helped these students gain greater social skills to achieve and maintain friendships with peers (Jones & Chiba, 1985). Sacks, Russell, Hirsh, Braden, and Gaylord-Ross (1991) used the Social Skills Assessment Tool to assess visually impaired students' level of social competence by examining whether they could interpret, generate, or apply sequences of social behaviors to a successful social encounter.

Given these perspectives, one can begin to establish a framework for developing effective procedures to provide social skills training to blind and visually impaired youngsters. However, the implementation of such strategies is highly dependent on the needs of the individual student and his or her ability to master the environment (conceptually, cognitively, and motorically), as well as on the development of social expectations from parents, teachers, and peers. There are ways to encourage and mediate positive social encounters. One must keep in mind, however, that these children's acquisition of such skills may not parallel that of sighted children and may require structured training.

THEORIES OF SOCIAL DEVELOPMENT

A solid theoretical foundation must be established to strengthen the rationale for developing strategies for training blind and visually impaired children in social skills. The following discussion evaluates five theories of social development—psychoanalytic, social identification, critical periods, social learning, and cognitive structural—in relation to the relative importance each attaches to interactions with peers and to their usefulness in helping blind and visually impaired children develop social competence.

The Psychoanalytic Model

Psychoanalytic theory emphasizes the centrality of the parent-child relationship in the child's early experiences. Its major proponents are Freud (1905/1974; 1924/1974; 1930/1974), Sullivan (1953), and Erikson (1950).

According to Freud, socialization occurs in early childhood when the child resolves the Oedipus complex by internalizing aggressive drives directed at the opposite-sex parent to form the superego. Since the child establishes a strong ego identity through the parent-child relationship, interactions with peers play a minimal role in early childhood, although they may help latency-aged children and adolescents solidify socially accepted behaviors. Unlike Freud, Sullivan emphasized the importance of social relationships in helping children develop a sense of self and understand others' needs and the importance of intimacy.

In Erikson's view, a child must experience parental control and support to advance through the eight stages of development to adulthood and old age. Although the family remains the child's central focus in later stages of childhood, he or she gains greater autonomy through interactions with others and experiences with objects in the environment.

Tait (1972), Fraiberg (1977), and Warren (1984) applied Erikson's model to blind and visually impaired children. They contended that these children are dependent on others to construct and integrate the external environment into a realistic, concrete world. However, Fraiberg noted that without intervention it is difficult for parents of young blind children to create an environment that fosters positive social interactions and physical stimulation and in which children are allowed to take risks. Therefore, the children may never master basic trust or autonomy and thus may never advance to higher stages of development.

Social Identification

In Durkheim's (1925/1973) theory of moral development, early familial experiences are the basis for later social development, but it is the child's experiences in the classroom that lead to a well-defined social identity. That is, the classroom teacher promotes activities that foster a team spirit and competition, group cohesiveness, and the internalization of an allegiance to society through the development of rules and group organization.

Blind and visually impaired children may find it difficult to identify with or develop an allegiance to a social group because of physical limitations and emotional constraints. In addition, they may be more directly influenced by the values and thoughts of adults than by those of the peer group.

Also, visually impaired children often must choose between identification with a sighted peer group or with a visually impaired peer group, and the social norms and values of each group may be different. For example, because society often perceives visually impaired people as being dependent, societal expectations for them may be less stringent.

Critical Periods

Harlow and Harlow's (1962) studies of primates demonstrated the importance of peer interaction in social development and substantiated the influence of "critical periods"—time frames in which an individual must learn particular behaviors that are crucial to advanced stages of development. Harlow and Harlow found that even when primates were given mother-infant experiences experimentally but were deprived of peer contact, their social adjustment as adults was delayed. Although there are no empirical data to substantiate such an effect in visually impaired children, observations of interactions between visually impaired and sighted individuals have described similar behavior (Santin & Nesker-Simmons, 1977). However, it is not possible to determine if such behavior is the result of insufficient maternal attachment; the lack of early intervention, including relationships with peers; or minimal neurological dysfunction that affects the visual system.

Social Learning Theory

Social learning theory incorporates the principles of learning theory (stimulus, response, reinforcement, and generalization). Its proponents contend that through observation, modeling, and feedback (Bandura, 1977; Bandura & Walters, 1963), children begin to discover what is acceptable behavior. Although adult or parental modeling takes place in early childhood, the power of peer interaction and modeling strongly affects the long-term socialization of the child. For example, Mischel (1966) demonstrated that children learn sex-related behaviors by observing, imitating, and modeling same-sex peers.

The concepts of social learning theory have widespread use as training models for visually impaired children. Since visually impaired children cannot simply imitate others' behaviors, they require physical modeling, verbal feedback, realistic reinforcement of their performance, and consistent instruction to reinforce behaviors (such as establishing eye contact) that depend on vision. Some effective training strategies (generalized procedures) have used nondisabled peers as trainers and role models to enhance the social skills of disabled youngsters (Chin-Perez et al., 1986; Gaylord-Ross, Haring, Breen, & Pitts-Conway, 1984; Strain, Cooke, & Appoloni, 1976; Strain & Odom, 1986; Voeltz, 1980, 1982).

Cognitive-Structural Theory

In cognitive-structural theory (Piaget, 1926/1959, 1932/1965), interactions with peers are necessary for social and cognitive development. During these interactions, such as play, children develop a sense of independence and cooperation and establish a set of rules for social behavior that help them move from heteronomy (dependence on numerous rules and sanctions set by adults) to autonomy.

Kohlberg (1969) developed a hierarchy of developmental stages, the movement through which is facilitated by interaction with peers. Children learn social conventions through increased role-taking experiences with adults and other children and through cognitive development.

Whereas Kohlberg believed that people are not able to distinguish between social conventions and moral reasoning until adolescence or adulthood, if then, Nucci and Turiel (1978) observed such reasoning in preschool children and concluded that it is imbedded in experiences with peers. Youniss and Volpe (1978) expanded this view of the influence of peer interactions to include not only role taking and cognitive growth, but the development of insight into the motivations of others in social situations.

According to the cognitive-structural model, the social development of blind and visually impaired children through interactions with peers may be impeded by the children's slower physical development and their reliance on sighted mediators' perceptions to make sense of the environment and to initiate positive social experiences. Thus, they may not have the locus of control to make judgments about individuals and objects that are outside their limited environments.

CONCLUSION

The theoretical perspectives outlined in this chapter clearly differ in the importance they place on the influence of interactions with peers on the social development of children. It is evident that they may not be adequate to explain the social development of children who are blind or visually impaired. One may argue that the social development of these children is dependent on a variety of experiences during their formative years and that, in order for independence to be encouraged, such experiences require the support and facilitation of parents, educators, and other children.

Thus, specific strategies to train blind and visually impaired children in social skills are as important as is experiential learning for the children's social development. Although empirical studies of the efficacy of these procedures for visually impaired children have been limited, the literature has established a framework for further investigation.

Chapter 2
Peer Interactions in Childhood: The Impact of Visual Impairment

Linda S. Kekelis

C ertain fundamental principles already discussed in the early pages of this book are of such importance that they bear repeating. Interactions with peers give children unique opportunities to develop and refine skills that are important for social development and acceptance by their peers. During such social exchanges, children learn how to gain access to play groups, engage in conversations, develop friendships, and resolve conflicts. Children who lack these skills are often ignored or rejected by their peers and may later develop psychological and physical problems.

Visual information plays an important role in the acquisition and refinement of skills that are critical for positive social interactions. Eye gaze regulates turn taking, gaze and gestures establish topics of conversation, smiles and gaze acknowledge and invite responses from partners, and contextual information enables children to monitor and respond to the interests of peers. For visually impaired children, the challenge of initiating and maintaining interactions with peers is considerable. Many children fail to master basic social skills and encounter rejection when mainstreamed with sighted children. Yet the literature contains few reports on the integration of visually impaired students in mainstream schools and its impact on social skills.

This chapter discusses the effects of visual impairment on interactions with peers in early childhood. It examines social interactions among sighted children to identify factors that contribute to social competence in childhood, identifies environmental factors that affect children's interactions and acceptance by peers, synthesizes and critiques research on visually impaired children's interactions with peers, reviews methods used to study and assess social interactions among children, and provides direction for future studies of the effects of visual impairment on children's interactions with peers.

The interactions of sighted children are discussed in detail in this chapter for a number of reasons. It is important for those who work with visually impaired children to know about the development of social skills and the importance of peer interactions in early childhood (Kekelis & Sacks, 1988). Sighted preschool-aged children do not predominantly engage in solitary or parallel play when in the company of peers. Educators and others who care for visually impaired children need to understand this fact, so they can provide sufficient opportunities for these children to interact with their peers. Such knowledge will also enable them to identify problems early enough to avoid long-term deficits in social skills in the children with whom they work. The studies of sighted children also provide important information on environmental factors that affect children's social interactions. Because children's social competence is *situation specific*, it is necessary to understand how different settings, activities, materials, and partners affect children's social interactions. One cannot expect that the development of sighted and visually impaired children will be identical or that environmental factors will affect the interactions of both groups in the same way, but an understanding of normal development is beneficial to work with blind and visually impaired children.

IMPORTANCE OF INTERACTIONS AMONG SIGHTED PEERS

Researchers have discovered that relationships with peers offer children unique opportunities to develop, practice, and refine interpersonal skills that are important for social development and acceptance by peers. During such interactions, children learn strategies for gaining access to ongoing play groups (Corsaro, 1985), attracting and directing the attention of other children

(Putallaz & Gottman, 1981), resolving conflicts (Shantz, 1986), engaging in fantasy play (Corsaro, 1985; Garvey, 1977), and maintaining friendships (Vaughn & Waters, 1981). Corsaro (1985, p. 121) described the differences between interactions with family members and those with peers:

> Within the family, children have relatively little opportunity for negotiation; they must recognize, accept, and adapt to their relationships with parents and siblings....Through interaction with peers, children learn that they can regulate social bonds on the basis of criteria that emerge from their personal needs and social contextual demands. They also learn that their peers will not always accept them immediately; often, a child must convince others of his merits as a playmate, and sometimes he must anticipate and accept exclusion.

The lack of acceptance by peers has been associated with a number of difficulties in childhood and adulthood: low school achievement (Bonney, 1971), delinquency (Roff, Sells, & Golden, 1972), and emotional and physical problems (Cowen, Petersen, Babigian, Izzo, & Trost, 1973). From both naturalistic observations and experimental probes, researchers have identified a number of factors that contribute to the acceptance of children by their peers (Coie & Kupersmidt, 1983; Dodge, 1983; Hartup, 1977; Hartup, Glazer, & Charlesworth, 1967; Putallaz & Gottman, 1981; Shantz, 1986).

Social Interactions during Infancy

Sighted children as young as 3 months display interest in their peers through visual gaze, smiling, touching, squealing, and pulling on peers. Lee (1973, cited in Rubin, 1980) found that infants in a day care center preferred the member of their play group who was responsive and friendly and least preferred the infant who was unfriendly, unresponsive, and belligerent.

Mueller (1972), Mueller and Brenner (1977), and Mueller and Rich (1976) observed that toddlers aged 12–16 months engaged in a number of socially directed behaviors with peers and that the social interactions became more complex as the toddlers got to know each other. The toddlers displayed greater friendliness toward one another and came together to interact, not simply to play with toys. Thus, children seem to require time with peers to develop coordinated social behaviors, and even those as young as 1 year old can benefit from participation in play groups.

Social Interactions during Childhood

Studies of interactions among preschool- and elementary-school-aged children have examined the children's social standing among classmates and the relationship between children's status and their social skills. One goal has been to identify factors that promote acceptance by peers and social adjustment and to provide direction for programs to train unskilled children in social skills.

In attempting to identify social skills that are critical for acceptance by peers, researchers have studied the interactions of children who are popular, rejected, or neglected by classmates. They have discovered that popular and unpopular children use different strategies for dealing with conflicts, joining play groups, and responding to peers' verbal and nonverbal behavior.

Dealing with Conflicts

The majority of studies of children's conflicts have concentrated on the rate of aggressive behavior displayed toward peers; their findings suggest only that unpopular children should engage in fewer displays of aggression. However, it is important for children to acquire skills to avoid conflicts or to resolve conflicts amicably.

Hatch (1984) found that kindergartners who were popular with peers had acquired strategies for saving face in the threat of conflicts. These children changed the subject, displayed tact and polite inattention, allowed others to make their expectations known, used modesty and hedging behaviors, offered explanations when they disagreed with others, and suggested alternative activities. Likewise, Sackin and Thelan (1984) discovered that the use of conciliatory behaviors to terminate conflicts allows preschool-aged children to reestablish positive relationships once the conflicts are resolved and hence to continue to play, whereas submission to peers during conflicts terminates the interactions. Children who are liked by their peers may use conciliatory behaviors to lessen the disruptiveness of conflicts. If so, those who work with rejected children need to do more than decrease the frequency of conflicts; they must teach these children skills that will allow them to continue to interact with peers after conflicts are resolved.

Conflicts among children vary in the extent to which verbal and physical aggression are used. To distinguish between the rate of participation in conflicts and the rate of aggressive behavior,

Shantz (1986) studied interactions of first- and second-grade children in play groups. Shantz defined conflict as an interaction in which two children disagree with each other and aggression as an act that involves verbal denigrations or physical harm resulting from such behaviors as biting, kicking, and shoving. Children who were initially disliked by members of their play group engaged more frequently in conflicts (cf. Dodge, 1983). In posttest ratings by peers, dislike was correlated more directly with the rate of conflict than with the rate of aggression. Thus, attempts to reduce unpopular children's use of physical aggression may not be sufficient; these children may also need to learn how to avoid engaging in conflicts in the first place.

Putallaz and Gottman (1981) noted that when popular children engaged in aggressive play, their peers responded more favorably to them than they did to unpopular children's aggressive behavior. The differential responses may be due to the physical attractiveness of popular children, the carryover effects of their status, or the manner in which the children engage in aggressive exchanges. Therefore, it is not sufficient to quantify the number of conflicts or aggressive exchanges in which children engage. Rather, the following factors must be considered: the children's personal characteristics, events leading to conflicts, previous interactional histories of children involved in conflicts, and the manner in which conflicts are resolved.

Gaining Entry to Peer Groups

In an ethnographic study of interactions among nursery school children, Corsaro (1979, 1985) found that young children often restrict the size of their play groups by rejecting peers' requests to join them. When a play group exceeds two or three children, sharing materials and play space and constructing play scenarios become unmanageable tasks, and the stability of the group is jeopardized.

Corsaro found that children were most effective in gaining entry into play groups when they used indirect means (circling the play group, producing similar behaviors as members of the play group, and nonverbally joining the group at play) that gave them the opportunity to gain information about the group's interests that they could use later to gain entry to the group. Children were less successful in gaining access to groups when they used direct strategies (greetings, requesting access, and asking questions) that disrupted the group's play and made it easy for its members to refuse them permission to enter.

Putallaz and Gottman (1979, cited in Putallaz & Gottman, 1981, 1982) found that popular second- and third-grade children used entry strategies that maximized the likelihood of being accepted, while unpopular children used those that were likely to be ignored or rejected. Popular children determined the "frame of reference" of the play group they wished to join and synchronized their entry attempts so that both their timing and themes were appropriate. When their initial attempts were ignored, they generated responsive second attempts that were generally successful. In contrast, unpopular children drew attention to themselves by stating their feelings, making statements about themselves, introducing new topics, asking informational questions, and disagreeing with members of the groups they wished to join; their approaches were generally unsuccessful.

The findings of Corsaro and of Putallaz and Gottman have considerable implications for those who try to improve the social standing of unpopular children. Without appropriate entry skills, these children are denied access to play and conversational exchanges of which they are desperately in need.

Dodge (1983) shed light on other differences between the social approaches of popular and unpopular children. Forty-eight previously unacquainted second-grade boys participated in play groups over eight sessions. Those who were considered most popular by other members of their play group at the end of the study had engaged in the *fewest* conversations with peers in the early sessions, but had participated in increasingly more conversations over time. In contrast, the rates of social exchanges of those children who were average, controversial, or rejected in their play groups were initially higher but did not increase over time, and those of children who were neglected decreased. Hence, it is crucial that children learn how to behave appropriately once they are accepted into play groups.

Responding to Peers

Children who are liked by their peers and who successfully enter play groups and participate in play and conversations with peers have learned to determine and respond to their peers' interests (Corsaro, 1985; Putallaz & Gottman, 1981). Charlesworth and Hartup (1967) stated that the frequency with which nursery school children reinforced their peers with responsive attention, approval, and affection was correlated with the frequency with which they received reinforcement.

In their study of the relationship between social status and social skills, Gottman, Gonso, and Rasmussen (1975) found that popular third- and fourth-graders provided more positive reinforcement than did unpopular children. They noted that children from different social classes used different types of reinforcement that were related to their social standing in the classroom: Children from mid- dle-income families used *verbal* reinforcement, whereas children from lower-income families used nonverbal reinforcement. Thus, social class and ethnicity should be taken into account in studies of children's social skills, particularly those in which children who need intervention are identified and given social-skills training.

Mueller (1972) found that young children not only showed inter- est in their peers but that most of their speech was acknowledged by their peers. Children were most likely to be responded to when their speech was responsive to their listener's previous turn and were likely to be ignored when their speech focused on their own activities.

Dodge (1983) discovered that popular children initially received significantly more positive responses than did unpopular children and received increasing amounts of positive responses over time. Rejected children received the least amount of positive responses from members of their play groups, while neglected children received decreasing amounts of positive responses. The degree to which children are responsive to their peers may, in part, be affected by the feedback provided by their immediate environment.

Personal Characteristics that Influence Social Standing

The majority of studies of children's social competence have focused on social skills that affect children's status among peers but have paid little attention to personal characteristics that may influence children's social standing. Both the production and per- ception of children's social behavior may be affected by their physical appearance, language skills, academic success, motor skills, gender, ethnicity, and social class.

Physical Attractiveness

Both children and adults evaluate children's sociability, behavior, academic ability, and social adjustment on the basis of their physical attractiveness (Bates, Morron, Pancsofar, & Sedlack, 1984; Dion, 1972; Dion, Berscheid, & Walster, 1972; Kleck, 1968). Dion (1972) discovered that adults considered unattractive children to be more likely than attractive children to commit transgressions, regarded their motives as dishonest, and thought their transgressions were more severe. These judgments are likely to affect children's self-perceptions and hence their interactions with peers. Langlois and Downs (1979) found that attractive and unattractive 3-year-olds did not differ in their displays of aggressive behavior, but that unattractive 5-year-olds displayed more aggressive behavior than did attractive ones. They noted (p. 416):

> Expectations for attractive and unattractive children may set a self-fulfilling prophecy into motion: unattractive children may be labeled as such and learn over time the stereotypes and behaviors associated with unattractiveness. Consequently, older children may exhibit aggressive behaviors consistent with this labeling and behave in accordance with others' expectations of them.

Academic and Athletic Abilities
Children's performance of academic and athletic tasks correlate with their social standing among their peers. Green, Forehand, Beck, and Vosk (1980, cited in La Greca & Stark, 1986) found that the academic achievement of third-grade students was related to positive ratings of interactions with peers. Similarly, Gottlieb, Semmel, and Veldman (1978) found that peers' evaluations of the academic performance of mentally retarded students correlated with their acceptance of the students. Furthermore, a number of studies have found a significant relationship between children's athletic abilities and their social standing among peers (Hops & Finch, 1983, cited in La Greca & Stark, 1986; McCraw & Tolbert, 1953, cited in Asher, Oden, & Gottman, 1977).

If only the social behaviors of unpopular children are targeted for intervention, some children may continue to be perceived as incompetent and less desirable companions. Thus, it may also be necessary to identify and highlight these children's talents or to help these children develop new skills.

Gender
In early childhood, children prefer same-sex friends and playmates (Asher, 1973; & Omark & Edleman, 1973, cited in Asher et al., 1977) not only because of differences in the activity levels and interests of boys and girls (Shure, 1963), but because of environ-

mental factors. When teachers have traditional views of masculine and feminine activities, boys and girls are less likely to play together (Bianchi & Bakeman, 1978). When teachers encourage boys to display nurturant behavior and support girls' interests in activities that are typically regarded as masculine, boys and girls may be more likely to enjoy each other's company. Children are more likely to choose playmates of the opposite sex when they attend small schools (Hallinan, 1979; Smith & Connolly, 1981, cited in Epstein, 1986). Epstein (1986) attributed this difference to the management techniques of teachers in small and large schools that may play a role in the extent to which boys and girls have opportunities to interact with one another. In addition, the extent to which boys and girls are reinforced for interacting with students of the opposite sex influences the frequency with which they develop cross-sex friendships (De Vries & Edwards, 1974; Serbin, Tonick, & Sternglanz, 1977, cited in Epstein, 1986).

Effects of Contextual Factors
Some researchers have looked at how contextual factors—activities, partners, settings, and materials—affect both the quantity and quality of interactions among children. By understanding the effects of these factors on social exchanges, educators can create environments that foster positive interactions among children.

Activities and Partners
The kinds of activities in which children participate have considerable impact on the amount and kind of interactions in which the children engage with peers. Vandenberg (1981) reported that during fine-motor activities, the preschool-aged children worked at tables with paper, pencils, paints, paste, and crayons and engaged in solitary or parallel play. During gross-motor activities, the children played with large blocks, slides, jungle gyms, and tumbling mats in larger groups and engaged in associative play, which is characterized by involvement around common activities.

Cook-Gumperz and Corsaro (1977) also discovered that the activities in which preschool children participate affected both the form and function of their interactions. Children engaged in elaborate role-play scenarios during activities in the playhouse, yet seldom described their actions. In sandboxes, they frequently described their actions because they had few expectations of the kinds of activities in which they would engage. During activities at the work tables, when the teacher controlled the flow and direction of the children's interactions, they engaged in little conversation. On the basis of these observed differences, Cook-Gumperz and Corsaro warned that it is not advisable to assess children's social competence during teacher-controlled activities.

Innocenti and his colleagues (1986) and Stamback and Verba (1986) also found that the presence of teachers or other adults affected children's social exchanges: Children engaged in the most peer interactions during free play when classroom teachers observed children's activities but did not engage in or direct the children's play. The number of peers who participate in activities influences children's interactions as well. In Borman's (1979) study, conversations were purposeful and mutually satisfying when two to four kindergartners participated in an activity, but when more than five or six children participated, the children had difficulty maintaining harmonious exchanges.

Type of Classroom
The milieu of the classroom can have a significant impact on interactions among peers. In classrooms in which students are encouraged to work together on academic work and are rewarded for their cooperative ventures, children are more likely to engage in social interactions that lead to reciprocated friendships. Under these circumstances, students are able to discover one another's talents and personalities and form satisfying relationships; there is also less likelihood that some students will be isolated (Hallinan, 1976; Hertz-Lazarowitz, Sharan, & Steinberg, 1980).

Materials
The number and types of toys that are available have considerable impact on the nature of children's interactions. The presence of many small toys seems to reduce the frequency of exchanges among peers, while the presence of large toys is more likely to increase it (DeStefano, 1976, cited in Vandell, Wilson, & Buchanan, 1980; Eckerman & Whately, 1977). Although the absence of toys increases the rate of peer interactions, it also increases unpleasant exchanges (Vandell et al., 1980).

PLACEMENT OF DISABLED CHILDREN IN MAINSTREAM CLASSROOMS
Legislation that mandates the education of disabled children in the least restrictive environment has brought children with learning, physical, and sensory impairments into regular education pro-

grams. The intent was to enrich the learning experiences of both disabled and nondisabled students. The success of these efforts must be measured not only by the academic achievements of disabled students but by social criteria. Only when disabled children have the opportunity to learn appropriate social behavior from and to develop positive relationships with nondisabled peers have integrated programs been truly effective.

For some disabled students, placement in regular education classrooms has resulted in increased social isolation and a more restrictive environment (Gottlieb & Budoff, 1973; Gresham, 1981; Hoben & Lindstrom, 1980). The lack of preservice training and of ongoing support for regular education teachers, along with the limited social, cognitive, and motor competencies of disabled students, often results in negative experiences. With the increasing trend toward mainstreaming, it is crucial that researchers and educators identify factors that contribute to the development of social competence in disabled children and their acceptance by nondisabled classmates.

Blind and visually impaired children are at a particular risk in mainstream education programs because visual information plays an important role in the acquisition and refinement of social skills that are necessary for acceptance by peers. Thus, they face a tremendous challenge when initiating and maintaining interactions with others (Andersen, Dunlea, & Kekelis, 1984; Andersen & Kekelis, 1983, 1985).

Despite the concern for social factors, there has been little in-depth study of the degree to which visually impaired children are integrated into mainstream programs, and guidelines to improve their participation have not been developed. The following sections discuss visually impaired children's interactions with adults and peers and programs to train these children in social skills, as well as theoretical and methodological concerns regarding research on visually impaired people.

DETERMINANTS OF SOCIAL INTERACTIONS WITH PEERS

Input of Others

Caregivers

Research on sighted children has documented the association between children's relationships with their caregivers and their later competence with peers (Lieberman, 1977). Numerous studies have demonstrated that blindness or visual impairment threatens the early attachment of many parents and their infants (Adelson, 1983; Als, 1982; Fraiberg, 1977; Friedman, 1986). It also affects the communication of parents and their children; without shared visual cues, including eye gaze, gestures, and smiles or contextual information, caregivers and visually impaired children often fail to notice, interpret, or respond appropriately to each other's attempts to communicate (Adelson, 1983; Als, 1982; Andersen & Kekelis, 1982; Fraiberg, 1977; Kekelis & Andersen, 1984; Rowland, 1984; Urwin, 1983).

As a result of these ineffective interactions early in their lives, some visually impaired children do not develop appropriate verbal and social skills and often have difficulty interacting with persons outside their families. They focus on their own interests and actions; ask numerous and repetitive questions; make an inordinate number of demands on their partners; abruptly shift topics; and are unresponsive to their partners' language, behavior, or concerns (Anderson & Kekelis, 1984, 1986; Chernus-Mansfield, Hayashi, & Kekelis, 1985; Kekelis & Chernus-Mansfield, 1984). These behaviors are likely to interfere with their ability to participate in conversations and play with peers. Throughout their six-year longitudinal study, Andersen and Kekelis (see, for example, Anderson & Kekelis, 1986; Andersen, Kekelis, & McGinnis, 1984; see also, Scott, 1969a) found that parents, teachers, and other adults often accommodated the inappropriate language and behavior of visually impaired children and did not require them to modify their behavior.

Classroom Teachers

Few studies have attempted to identify factors in the classroom environment that affect interactions between visually impaired students and sighted classmates. Those studies that have done so discovered that the input of classroom teachers has considerable influence on both the quantity and the quality of peer interactions.

Workman (1986) examined the effects of teachers' input on peer interactions with four visually impaired preschoolers. Input that was found to enhance visually impaired children's interactions with their peers included (1) *descriptions of the social environment* that provided information about the roles and activities of peers, (2) *direct prompts* that suggested roles to take and actions to perform, and (3) *indirect prompts* that were directed to the sighted classmates. Input by classroom teachers that hindered peer interactions included descriptions of the physical environment, such as statements about the locations of persons and objects in the classroom. Kekelis and Andersen (1984) found that parents of visually impaired children frequently simplified their input and described the physical environment because of the lack of visual cues. Teachers may respond in a similar manner and therefore may need to learn that such descriptions may interfere with peer interactions in the classroom.

Workman also discovered that during group activities, interactions between visually impaired children and their classmates were infrequent when classroom teachers did not directly work with the group in which the visually impaired students participated. Therefore, if the mainstreaming experience of the visually impaired student is to be optimal, classroom teachers must make social interactions a priority.

Efforts to mainstream six kindergarten and first-grade visually impaired students were reported to be most positive when both the classroom and the special education teachers regarded the primary goal of the mainstreaming experience to be social and when they actively involved the visually impaired students in classroom activities and conversations (Kekelis & Sacks, 1988). These findings are presented in detail in Chapter 4.

Peers

Unlike adults, peers are often less able or willing to accommodate the inappropriate and ambiguous speech or inappropriate behavior of visually impaired children (Andersen & Kekelis, 1986). Their unwillingness may provide the impetus for the children to rethink and revise their assumptions about language and social behavior.

Despite the importance of input from peers, many young visually impaired children do not have the same opportunities to interact with peers as do sighted children; their parents either lack the resources to arrange for such interactions, find them stressful because of the differences between their children's development and that of sighted children, or wish to avoid the stares and tactless comments of strangers (Chernus-Mansfield, Hayashi, Horn, & Kekelis, 1985). Furthermore, many blind and visually impaired children are involved in home-based early-intervention programs that focus on the development of the parent-child relationship.

Those who are in center-based programs are often provided with services to remedy motor, language, and cognitive deficits, which leaves little time to address social needs.

Thus, once visually impaired children are in programs with sighted peers, they may not be able to take advantage of the opportunity because of deficits in social skills. For example, Hoben and Lindstrom (1980) found that visually impaired students in grades 1–12 initiated fewer interactions; responded less to their classmates than did their sighted peers; and, according to their classroom teachers, spent more instructional time alone and waited to be approached by their classmates.

In their social-skills training program for disabled students, Jones and Chiba (1985) discovered that visually impaired children were rejected by classmates more than were other groups of disabled elementary school students. These students were rated positively by peers who were themselves unpopular with their peers (Jones, Lavine, & Shell, 1972); since it is likely that such classmates were isolated and deficient in social skills, they probably were not optimal partners for visually impaired children (Centers & Centers, 1963).

Therefore, the quality of input from peers is important for the social development and well-being of visually impaired children. It is not sufficient that these children simply interact with others; they must engage in social exchanges that maximize their social development. As Kekelis (1988b) observed, many of the social interactions between a blind kindergartner and his sighted classmates were negative and did little to advance the boy's social development. The sighted classmates often teased the blind boy by calling out his name and then running away when he attempted to find them. It seemed that they did not know how to get beyond greetings and requests for names—a phenomenon also noted in interactions between visually impaired children and their adult caregivers (Kekelis, 1981; Kekelis & Andersen, 1984).

Studies of the social skills of blind and visually impaired children have focused solely on the children's interactions with sighted peers. However, it is also important to provide the children with opportunities to interact with other visually impaired children. Contacts with peers who are experiencing similar challenges in mainstream settings may help them learn to cope with problems they face in interactions with sighted peers (Harrell & Curry, 1987).

Skills of Visually Impaired Children

Play Skills

Young children spend much of their time together in play. Thus, although it is not enough for visually impaired children to learn how to gain access to peer groups if they do not have adequate play skills, surprisingly little attention has been paid to the development of play skills in these children. One such study of visually impaired children aged 20 months to 4 years, 4 months (Parsons, 1986) found that the children not only engaged in less functional play (using toys for their intended purpose) and more stereotypic play (mouthing, banging, and waving toys), but frequently wandered away from their toys and tried to engage adults in interactions. When visually impaired children lack the play skills necessary to participate in interactions with classmates, it is critical that classroom teachers teach them how to play in a systematic manner and that they carefully monitor the children's attempts to try out these skills with their sighted classmates.

Language Skills

Visual impairment affects language development in a number of ways. Visually impaired children use more echolalic speech than do their sighted peers (Chernus-Mansfield et al., 1985; Dunlea, 1989; Fraiberg, 1977; Prizant, 1987). When their language is related to past experiences, rather than to the ongoing activities of their peers, it leads to breakdowns in communication and may eventually influence their social standing among their classmates.

Visually impaired children ask more questions than do sighted children and more questions that are irrelevant to the activities that take place around them (Chernus-Mansfield et al., 1985; Erin, 1986; Mulford, 1983). The questions they ask may limit their opportunities to enter play groups and to engage in sustained exchanges with peers.

The language of visually impaired children focuses more frequently on the children's activities, possessions, and feelings and is less responsive to the interests of their partners than is the speech of sighted children (Andersen & Kekelis, 1984; Dunlea, 1989). These differences may affect both the quantity and quality of feedback from peers.

Social Skills

Little research has focused on the manner in which blind and visually impaired children deal with conflicts, enter play groups, and respond to peers. If teachers are to train visually impaired children to become socially competent, they must understand how the children acquire and display social skills.

In Kekelis and Sacks's study (1988), the blind child who was liked by his classmates and teachers showed that he liked his classmates and was interested in their activities and feelings; his outgoing personality attracted the attention and involvement of others. However, even with his social skills, he required considerable assistance from teachers to demonstrate his competence in exchanges with classmates.

A blind preschooler in Kekelis's (1988a) study did not ask questions about her classmates, did not request to sit beside any classmate during snack or circle time, and did not respond when classmates demonstrated positive feelings toward her. Although her classmates reinforced each other by paying compliments, requesting assistance, and providing evidence of their concern, she did not willingly interact with anyone. Thus, blind and visually impaired children may need to be taught how to demonstrate affection and attachment to peers.

Motor Skills

Visual impairment often delays the acquisition and refinement of motor skills during childhood (Fraiberg, 1977). Without adequate instruction in orientation and travel techniques, blind children may have difficulty moving about their classrooms. Sighted peers are sometimes asked to guide visually impaired classmates in classrooms. This responsibility can become a burden when these children's mobility skills are poor. Furthermore, with the open spaces of playgrounds and the quick pace of activities, it may be particularly difficult for visually impaired children to participate in activities with peers during recess.

Academic Competence

Although academic success is the primary concern of most classroom and resource-room teachers, little is known about the achievement of blind and visually impaired children in mainstream educational programs. The relationship between these children's academic success and acceptance by peers has not been addressed.

Contextual Variables

An important outcome of the ethnographic study by Kekelis and Sacks (1988) was the identification of contextual variables that affected interactions between blind and visually impaired children and their classmates in mainstream educational programs. While such factors as seating arrangements, composition of play groups, and the social milieu of the classroom affected sighted classmates, the extent to which these factors influenced the social experience of visually impaired students was considerable and, at times, meant the difference between social isolation and involvement in classroom activities.

SOCIAL-SKILLS TRAINING

Programs to train visually impaired persons in social skills have targeted mainly adolescents and adults (see Van Hasselt, 1983b, for a review). Van Hasselt, Hersen, Kazdin, Simon, & Mastantuono (1983) developed training packages to improve visually impaired clients' posture, facial expressions, gaze, assertiveness, gestures, and speech. In addition, a number of researchers (Farkas, Sherick, Matson, & Loebig, 1981; Petersen, Austin, & Lang, 1979; Sanders & Goldberg, 1977; Yarnall, 1979) have used reinforcements and prompts to increase social skills. Although these programs have addressed the needs of older clients, they will be discussed here because their approaches are being modeled by those who work with young visually impaired children.

Role-Play Assessments

Role-play tests have been used to identify behaviors in need of treatment and to evaluate the effectiveness of treatments (see, for example, Van Hasselt et al., 1983). During these tests, clients are instructed to pretend that the simulated situations are actually occurring. Since individuals differ in their ability to visualize imaginary scenes and to respond naturally, instructing clients to respond realistically to prompts does not ensure that they will. Furthermore, although role-play scenarios guarantee that clients receive identical stimuli during training, they create a contextual vacuum. In real interactions, partners monitor one another's behavior, receive verbal and nonverbal feedback, and make adjustments as interactions progress. The less natural the experimental situation, the less likely it is that participants will behave in a natural manner that is representative of their typical performance (Bellack, 1983). Thus, it is essential that training programs for blind and visually impaired individuals are conducted within the context of interactions that occur in the natural environment.

Selection of Behaviors

In the majority of programs, inadequate justification has been provided for the behaviors that are targeted for training. Although the appropriate use of gaze, posture, and facial expressions and the ability to assert oneself are important in social exchanges, there is no evidence that such behaviors are more critical for the social adjustment and well-being of visually impaired clients than are other, nontargeted behaviors.

To date, there has been no in-depth study of the social interactions of blind adults. As a result, little is known about the range and subtlety of behaviors that impact on blind individuals' social interactions.

Programs for Children

In the social-skills training program conducted by Jones and Chiba (1985), visually impaired children received instruction in how to meet others, sharing and helping, the importance of friends and of trust and reciprocity among friends, the impact of arguments on friendships, and how friends resolve arguments. Training involved listening to videotapes of children modeling appropriate social behaviors and role playing the skills targeted for intervention. After treatment, Jones and Chiba found no significant improvements in the children's sociometric statuses, concepts of friendship, role-play behaviors, or social behaviors. They concluded that visually impaired children may require significantly more contact with peers to change their behavior and social standing. Clearly, training in social skills must include a more direct approach than listening to tapes and role playing. Furthermore, the social behaviors that are targeted for intervention must be ones that affect the interactions and acceptance of visually impaired students.

Using nondisabled peers to teach socially appropriate play behavior to visually impaired children with multiple disabilities, Sisson, Van Hasselt, Hersen, and Strain (1985) reported gains in the participants' initiations of social interaction and social responses to peers that were maintained at a four-month follow-up.

Sacks (1987) and Sacks and Gaylord-Ross (1989) used peers and teachers to teach social skills to visually impaired children in elementary school. Social behaviors that were targeted for intervention were determined with the input of the visually impaired students and their teachers. Training addressed the direction of gaze, body posture, positive initiations, and the joining of peer groups and sharing in group activities. It involved modeling, the use of prompts, discussions of the need for the desired social behaviors, and role play. After the four-week program, the following results were noted: (1) peer-mediated training produced improvements in social behaviors that were maintained over time and generalized to the natural setting and (2) teacher-directed training produced improvements in social behaviors that declined in the follow-up and were not generalized in the natural setting. In addition, Sacks (1987) reported improvements in measures of social validation among the visually impaired students who received her training package. For example, these students were more likely to be regarded as desirable playmates by nondisabled classmates.

THEORETICAL AND METHODOLOGICAL ISSUES

Studies of social interactions among children have a number of shortcomings in the manner in which social competence is conceptualized and in the methods by which peer interactions are observed and analyzed. The critique that follows is intended to provide direction for future studies of blind and visually impaired children and to alert those who make use of research findings for assessing and training these children in social skills.

Selection of Social Behaviors for Examination

Studies of interactions among children focus on behaviors that occur frequently. Although these behaviors have considerable repercussions on children's social standing among peers, other events that occur with less frequency may also be significant. For example, in a study of omega children (children who are verbally neglected and isolated members of their peer groups), Garnica (1981) discovered that these children were subjected to taunts, teasing, and insults from peers only when they challenged their status. If Garnica had considered only the frequency of such negative responses, she might have concluded that omega children were not victimized by their peers. If she had examined only the rate of assertive behaviors displayed by these children, she might have concluded that the children needed to become more assertive. Only by examining in detail the rare occasions in which omega children tried to gain the attention of their peers did Garnica discover the true social standing of omega children and the danger these children faced when they challenged their standing among peers with the kinds of behaviors that most children use to express their needs.

Timing and Quality of Social Behaviors

In addition to investigating differences in the rates of social behaviors of popular and unpopular children, it is also important to look for subtle differences in these children's behaviors. For instance, both the timing and quality of social behaviors need to be considered when one evaluates children's social competence in peer exchanges. Peers may respond differently to a display of aggressive behavior, depending on whether it is justified (when it is a response to unfair provocation) or unjustified (when it arises out of the blue). Even a request for clarification, which is generally regarded as positive, can be considered inappropriate if it interrupts the children's interactions.

Determinants of Peer-Directed Social Behaviors

Children's interactions with their peers are typically studied in isolation from their interactions and relationships with others. Investigators look for explanations of children's social standing in social behaviors that can be immediately observed. Although such an approach provides clear-cut correlational findings, it limits the understanding of children's social development.

Family-Associated Factors

Numerous family-associated factors contribute to children's social standing among their peers: children's attachment to their mothers (Lieberman, 1977) and the parents' educational level, socioeconomic status, intelligence, and attitudes toward caregiving (Roff et al., 1972). Visual impairment affects the attachment of infants and caregivers (Fraiberg, 1977; Friedman, 1986) and later interactions within the family.

Cultural and Societal Factors

A variety of cultural and societal factors affect the frequency and quality of interactions with peers: the presence of other persons, the setting in which interactions occur, the number of children in a family, the amount of work that a mother is required to perform and the amount of assistance she receives, the roles assigned to children in their families, and the social behaviors in which caregivers engage. Much of the research on the social competence of both nondisabled and disabled children has been conducted on middle-class white samples. Studies of other social classes and ethnic groups have found differences in the children's social development (Gottman et al., 1975).

Observations across Settings

The majority of studies of peer interactions have examined social exchanges among classmates. However, since children spend as much time interacting with peers in their neighborhoods, after-school programs, and clubs and at home, it is likely that their interactions in these settings will have a significant impact on their social competence and well-being. It should be kept in mind that the reactions of strangers may make it more difficult for some parents to arrange for their blind or visually impaired children to interact with peers in the neighborhood and community.

Value of a Holistic Approach

Researchers have relied on a traditional hypothesis-testing method to identify factors that correlate with children's social standing among their peers. Their efforts have identified children at risk and have targeted a number of social skills to train, but their approach typically addresses a limited number of issues—and only in the short term.

An ethnographic approach may be useful in discovering new and significant factors that affect blind and visually impaired children's social encounters. Rather than impose predetermined research questions, ethnographers allow research inquiries to arise from observations made throughout their investigations (Schatzman & Strauss, 1973).

Need for a Long-Term Approach

Because of the short-term approach used by most researchers, little is known about the development of skills that are important for acceptance by peers. How do popular children learn communication and play skills that make them desirable play partners, and how do they use feedback from their peers to refine their interactive skills? While investigators have looked at the short-term stability of peer ratings, how stable are these ratings throughout childhood? How do withdrawn and rejected children attempt to modify their social standing? These questions have not been adequately addressed.

It is especially important that teachers who attempt to improve the social skills of visually impaired children take a long-term approach. The majority of training programs in social skills are conducted for only a few sessions; improvements are typically reported immediately after training; and follow-ups, if done, are generally conducted days or weeks later. However, to be significant, changes in social skills must be maintained for longer periods than those currently evaluated in most programs.

Environmental Factors

With the demands for mainstreaming disabled students, it is crucial that environmental factors that contribute to or hinder blind and visually impaired children's development of social competence and integration in groups of sighted peers are identified. On the basis of such research, intervention programs could address the unique needs of children in mainstream educational programs.

Dangers of a Comparative Approach

Researchers base their research questions and methods of collecting and analyzing samples of social behaviors on studies of nondisabled children. It is dangerous to rely solely on a comparative approach because the norms from data collected from sighted children may not be appropriate for blind or visually impaired children, whose special needs may be overlooked in the process and whose within-group differences are likely to be overlooked. Visually impaired children are a heterogenous population with differences in etiology, age of onset of the visual impairment, degree of visual loss, and presence of concomitant disabilities. Therefore, they may require a variety of approaches to social-skills training that are sensitive to their needs. Rather than compare the social behaviors of visually impaired and sighted children, it may be more useful to contrast those of low- and high-functioning visually impaired children to determine how to promote their optimal social development and well-being (Raver & Drash, 1988).

CONCLUSION

Interactions with peers provide sighted children with unique opportunities to develop and refine interpersonal skills that are critical for social development and acceptance. Visual information plays an important role in the acquisition and refinement of these skills. For blind and visually impaired children, the challenge of interacting with peers is considerable, and many face rejection when mainstreamed with sighted students. Therefore, it is surprising that researchers have paid little attention to blind and visually impaired children's development of social skills or to the nature of their interactions with peers. Recent studies indicate that it is difficult for blind and visually impaired children and their peers to engage in conversations and play without considerable assistance from classroom teachers and special education instructors. The effects of environmental variables, including partners, materials, activities, and settings, have only begun to be addressed. If researchers and educators are to perform meaningful assessments of blind and visually impaired children and are to implement effective interventions, it is imperative that in-depth, long-term ethnographic studies of these children's interactions with their peers, and the many factors that influence these interactions, are conducted.

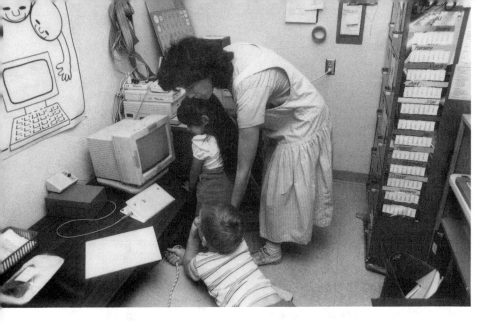

Part 2: Research

The findings of research on social-skills training have been used to develop strategies for teaching a variety of disabled persons in school and community programs. However, little research has been conducted with visually impaired children, particularly in naturalistic environments. The chapters in Part 2 describe studies that illustrate different research approaches that may be used in schools, at home, and in the community to teach social skills. These approaches are the ethnographic (qualitative) approach, the traditional behavioral approach, and the peer-mediated approach.

Ethnographic methods allow researchers to observe the environment or culture of the targeted person or community over time. The studies reported in Chapters 3, 4, and 5 used these methods to understand the socialization process of mainstreamed visually impaired students and to examine the interactions of visually impaired children and their teachers and sighted classmates. This approach yielded striking and similar results, even though the studies were conducted independently and in vastly different economic, social, and cultural environments. The observational techniques employed established criteria to maximize the social integration of students with visual impairments, including strategies for effective educational placement, the use of peers as models and facilitators in the regular classroom, and ideas to heighten sighted students' and teachers' awareness of the individual needs of visually impaired students.

The study presented in Chapter 6 is a comparative analysis of the long-term effectiveness and generalizability of a teacher-directed intervention versus a peer-mediated social-skills training approach. Both strategies can be used effectively by teachers in an array of educational settings. In the first strategy, the visually impaired students received training from a teacher, who used traditional behavioral intervention, including instruction, modeling of the targeted behavior, role playing, rehearsal, verbal and gestural feedback, and homework. In the second strategy, sighted age-mates received training from the authors and acted as "special friends" to the visually impaired students. Their direct instruction of the visually impaired students was much less structured than in the teacher-directed intervention, focusing on mutually determined play activities, into which targeted behaviors were infused. Once the students became comfortable with each other, the sighted peers provided positive and negative (realistic) feedback to their visually impaired friends. Although the quality of the training may not have been as sophisticated or precise as in the teacher-directed intervention, the data clearly showed the strength of the peer- mediated intervention, especially with respect to the carryover of skills acquired during training to naturalistic environments. More important, the visually impaired students maintained a relatively high level of social competence in subsequent observations.

The research methods described in Part 2 can be employed by both parents and professionals. Qualitative interventions make it possible to observe and to understand further the dynamics of the social networks of visually impaired children and youths. Through observational analyses, we can begin to design strategies that promote positive social experiences for students with visual impairments at home and in school and community settings. The use of peers as facilitators of social-skills instruction for visually impaired children seems to add to the long-term effectiveness of such an approach. Although the peer-mediated approach is not always the best method of instruction, peers provide valuable insights into the social culture and interactive process for their visually impaired counterparts.

It should be noted that the names of people and places in the chapters in this section, as elsewhere in this book, have been changed to protect the privacy of the individuals concerned. Although they use different research approaches, the chapters taken together point toward certain conclusions: It is essential that the teacher of visually impaired students be more involved on a routine basis in mainstreaming efforts, that difficulties created in this area by the prevailing shortage of such teachers be addressed, and that thought and care be exercised in the selection of regular classroom teachers—and classmates—of visually impaired children. It is hoped that these chapters will stimulate readers to try the research approaches described on an informal everyday basis with individual children with whom they work.

Chapter 3
A Field Study of a Blind Preschooler

Linda S. Kekelis

This study used an ethnographic approach to examine in detail one blind child's interactions with her classmates. Its goals were (1) to identify factors that affect blind and visually impaired children's interactions with their peers, (2) to generate hypotheses for future studies of blind and visually impaired children, and (3) to develop a set of preliminary guidelines that practitioners can use to promote positive social interactions between sighted children and visually impaired children.

An ethnographic study approach was used to collect and analyze data simultaneously. Although the project was begun with a set of general hypotheses, new questions arose during the study and were investigated. With this open-ended study approach, the research issues were not imposed on the data, but emerged from the observations. This technique led to the discovery of issues that are of special importance to visually impaired children and generated hypotheses for future investigations. The study of Ashley was conducted over a four-month period; two to three visits were scheduled with her each week.

PARTICIPANTS

Ashley
Ashley Addison, who was 3 1/2 years old when the study began, had an active interest in the persons and objects in her surround-

ings and a creative imagination that she used to entertain herself and engage others in social interactions. During my first visit to her home, Ashley displayed none of the social and linguistic deficits that are common in blind and visually impaired children. She attracted her parents' attention with appropriate formulas such as "You know what?"; did not ask irrelevant questions or behave inappropriately; and expressed her ideas in creative sentences, rather than in formulaic speech.

Ashley was sighted until age 6 months, when she was physically abused and violently shaken by a baby-sitter. As the result of the trauma, the retinas of both her eyes detached, leaving her with no useful vision. Her parents received disparate reports on Ashley's condition. Several ophthalmologists told them that her visual functioning would eventually improve, but it did not.

Ashley returned home from the hospital with the competencies of a 2-month-old. Despite this early setback, she quickly reacquired language, cognitive, and motor skills. At 16 months, she was enrolled in a preschool program for blind and visually impaired children. This placement eased Mrs. Addison's anxiety and guilt because she felt confident leaving Ashley in the care of the highly competent staff. The program's instructors reassured Mrs. Addison that Ashley was not developmentally delayed, but was, in fact, advanced for a child with a vision loss.

Throughout this period, the family received educational services and emotional support from a home-based intervention program for blind and visually impaired children and their families. This program helped the Addisons develop realistic expectations for Ashley and gave them reading materials on blindness. The following summer and thereafter, Ashley attended the Sunshine Program, a preschool morning program for sighted children operated by a neighborhood Jewish community center. Although the family was not Jewish, they selected the program because they liked its child-centered curriculum. At age 3, Ashley was also enrolled in the Blind Children's Program (BCP), a preschool morning program for blind and visually impaired children that provided mobility and prebraille instruction. She attended the BCP two days a week and the Sunshine Program three days a week.

Her caregivers described Ashley as strong-willed and, at times, stubborn. These qualities were manifested both positively and negatively. Ashley frequently asserted her independence with the command, "Let me do it by myself!" and often mastered new skills through trial and error. However, she sometimes refused to cooperate in required school activities and defied her caregivers' reasonable requests, just as her sighted classmates did. The expression of these personality traits depended, in part, upon the responses of Ashley's parents, teachers, and peers.

Ashley's humor and imagination also served as both strengths and weaknesses. Playing with sounds, changing people's names, and playing make-believe were her favorite activities. Children and adults sometimes responded to these activities positively, but at other times they responded negatively because the activities prevented meaningful play and conversations.

The Addisons

The Addisons were an upper-middle-class Caucasian family that valued intelligence, creativity, and independence in children. Mr. Addison was an administrator of a large hospital with a busy work schedule, but he maintained a close relationship with Ashley.

Mrs. Addison was the children's primary caregiver. An articulate and reflective person, she had developed a thorough understanding of Ashley's special needs. She used language and hands-on experiences to expand Ashley's understanding of her environment and encouraged Ashley to be a creative and independent problem solver.

Jake, Ashley's younger brother, was 1 year old when the study began. He had a likable temperament, curiosity, and the ability to entertain himself. Jake was a positive addition to the Addison family and provided Ashley with opportunities to help a less competent partner, to share possessions and the attention of adults, and to develop skills that would help her play with her peers.

SETTINGS AND ACTIVITIES

To gain as complete an understanding of Ashley's world as possible, I observed her in a variety of settings, including her home, a swimming class, a gymnastics class, a field trip to a library, the Sunshine Program, and the BCP. The majority of observations were made at Ashley's preschool, the Sunshine Program.

Sunshine Program

Ashley's classmates at the Sunshine Program included 22 children, aged 3 and 4, who came from middle- and upper-class families. Although the program was operated by a Jewish community center, many of the children enrolled were not Jewish. Despite the children's different personalities, temperaments, and social skills, they engaged in a significantly higher rate of interaction with classmates than did Ashley.

The overall sizes of the Sunshine and BCP classrooms were comparable. However, the Sunshine Program had a much larger outdoor play area with two swing sets, a large sandbox, several climbing structures; automobile and truck tires to climb; tables for water play and baking activities; and large, wide-open spaces in which the children ran and rode bicycles. This outdoor play area afforded the sighted students innumerable places to run, hide, and play imaginatively, but it proved to be a restrictive environment for Ashley. Ashley was aware of some of the materials that were available in the yard, but she could not independently move around the grounds because its landmarks were far apart. She could have benefited from mobility instruction in this outdoor area, but mobility lessons were provided only at the BCP. Although the techniques she learned at the BCP were valuable, they would have been more meaningful if Ashley had been taught a path that was important in her day-to-day activities.

In the Sunshine Program, the children were self-directed. They had considerable freedom to select activities and a variety of options from which to choose. The size of the playground, number of classmates, and availability of toys enabled Ashley's classmates to engage in numerous activities. During unstructured play time, the teachers monitored the children's activities and responded to the children in a nondirective manner. They often set up activities, such as water tables, easels and paints, and clay. This arrangement accommodated the children's individual needs. Some children enjoyed large groups, whereas others liked small groups or to play alone; some enjoyed indoor activities, whereas others preferred gross-motor activities outdoors; and some liked to draw and paint, whereas others preferred building with blocks.

Each day also included a number of routines and structured activities in which the children were expected to participate. At the start of each day, the children gathered in a circle to sing songs, listen to the day's schedule, and share conversations. After outdoor play, they returned to the classroom for snack time. Later, they participated in more free play, art activities, show-and-tell, and story time.

Special activities and materials were offered to the children each day. However, the teachers sometimes described them in a manner that may have been difficult for Ashley to comprehend. Daily agendas were discussed at snack time when the children were absorbed in conversation and eating, were shouted across the outdoor playground while the children were running and yelling, and were announced in songs. Even if the sighted students failed to hear these announcements, they could see the toys and activities. Without visual cues, Ashley may have missed a number of opportunities to participate in activities with her classmates because she did not know they were available.

Overall, the Sunshine Program was not designed for a visually impaired child. Its layout and class size made it difficult for Ashley to be independent and to engage in interactions with her classmates. Recognizing this fact, the program director admitted Ashley under the condition that an aide would be provided to protect Ashley's safety and to keep the teachers' attention from being diverted from the sighted students. A student enrolled in the Department of Special Education of a local college volunteered for the position. The aide primarily served as Ashley's attendant, but she also rotated with the classroom teachers so her service did not set Ashley apart from her classmates. During the field study, the children did not make any comments to suggest they were aware the aide was in their class primarily to assist Ashley. They frequently approached the aide and asked for her assistance and involved her in their activities.

BCP

At the BCP, Ashley had four classmates—three boys and one girl. Her classmates were between the ages of 3 and 5, and their vision loss ranged from severe visual impairment to total blindness. The two older boys were highly verbal and mobile and engaged in some interactions with Ashley. The younger boy was language delayed and severely emotionally disturbed. The other girl was developmentally delayed and engaged in a great deal of echolalic speech; although her language and social skills were rapidly developing as the result of the program's stimulation, they were not comparable to Ashley's, and the two girls did not often converse or play together.

The activities at the BCP were more structured and teacher directed than were those at the Sunshine Program. Teaching occurred both individually and in small groups. The classroom environment was set up for blind and visually impaired children, and the toys, books, and other learning materials were kept in consistent locations. Ashley was expected to travel independently in the classroom and on the playground, although adult supervision was always provided.

The classroom teacher recognized the importance of peer interactions for her students and was adept at encouraging them. Ashley engaged in some positive peer interactions in this program, but she spent a large amount of time playing by herself or engaging in lessons and conversations with the staff. Perhaps if there had been a more competent girl in the class Ashley would have conversed and played more with a peer.

Participation in Two Programs

Neither preschool program could meet all Ashley's needs. Concerned with the lack of appropriate peer models at the BCP, the Addisons looked for an alternative placement. They were encouraged to enroll Ashley in the Sunshine Program by its staff. The Addisons hoped that this program would give Ashley the opportunity to form friendships with sighted children and to learn skills from appropriate role models.

Ashley's participation in the Sunshine Program was helpful to Mrs. Addison, who sometimes doubted Ashley's overall competence. Mrs. Addison saw that the sighted children also had difficulty separating from their mothers, had temper tantrums and crying fits, and sometimes refused to share and cooperate with their peers. These observations helped her to put Ashley's problems into perspective.

Participation in two programs on alternate days appeared to have some drawbacks. At the BCP, in particular, Ashley seemed to be a minor participant in classroom activities. She missed many of its weekly activities and did not share the same background experiences as her classmates. At the Sunshine Program, she was enrolled long after the other children had established relationships with each other.

Despite the shortcomings of the placements, Ashley had positive experiences in both programs, which often complemented each other. With the help of her teachers, she developed a number of skills that were important for her future relationships with peers.

RESEARCH METHODS

Observations

BCP

During the study, I spent several mornings each week at the BCP observing Ashley and conducting an intervention with one of Ashley's classmates (see Kekelis, 1986a). During class time, I observed routines, took notes, and audiotaped Ashley's interactions. I followed Ashley from place to place but attempted to remain as unobtrusive as possible. Often, I sat on the classroom floor in an area adjacent to Ashley and her classmates. My participation in this setting was intentionally limited because there were so many adults in the classroom—the head instructor, two teacher's aides, a speech therapist, and a mobility instructor. Since it was not easy for the head teacher to maintain order—given the diversity of personalities, agendas, and comings and goings of adults—it was critical that I did not add to the stimulation in the classroom.

Sunshine Program

At the Sunshine Program, Ashley was observed one morning each week during the first two months of the study and two mornings a week during the last month. To fit into the Sunshine Program, I adopted a different role than at the BCP. The physical dimensions and size of the classroom allowed for more opportunities to participate in activities. In fact, Ashley's classmates demanded that I do more than observe and record their interactions with Ashley. They asked me questions, requested my permission and assistance in their games, and shared their feelings and ideas with me. Their responsiveness and interest encouraged me to participate in their social world. When several of the children asked why I was taking notes, I told them I was learning about their play—an explanation that seemed to satisfy them. During my visits, I tried not to single out Ashley and, in fact, interacted more with Ashley's classmates than with her. Ashley preferred the company of adults to that of her peers, and I did not want to encourage her to talk or play with me.

Ashley's Home

Ashley was observed at home on three occasions, and the observations were revealing about her underlying competence and the kinds of expectations her mother had for her. The teachers at the

Sunshine Program used these expectations to develop their goals for Ashley. These visits also yielded information about Ashley's history.

Visits to the Addisons served another important function. Mrs. Addison was interested in Ashley's progress in both school programs, but she had little opportunity to observe Ashley at either site. Ashley went to and from the BCP by school bus. Mrs. Addison drove Ashley to the Sunshine Program and stayed for approximately 10 minutes each school day; she had little opportunity to observe interactions between Ashley and her classmates because Ashley remained by her side while she was there. The observations that were made at both schools were discussed with the Addisons at home.

Note Taking

During visits to Ashley's schools, condensed notes describing Ashley's interactions with classmates and teachers were taken, and an expanded account was written after each visit. The account included observational notes, which described the who, what, when, and how of events; theoretical notes, which were interpretive and hypothesis generating; and methodological notes, which reflected observational techniques (see Schatzman & Strauss, 1973).

Initially, the notes summarized events in the classrooms. Later, a number of themes emerged that appeared critical to the development of Ashley's social competence. Once these themes were identified, they became the focus of attention during visits to the schools.

Interviewing

Talking about Ashley with her mother and teachers shed light on their behavior and on Ashley's underlying competence and performance. These interviews helped explain the reasons for the discrepancy between Ashley's competence in interactions with adults and her lack of competence in the company of peers. Aside from incidental discussions throughout the project, longer and more formal interviews with Ashley's mother and teachers were scheduled during the final weeks of the project. By this time, the teachers knew me well and understood the kinds of concerns that interested me. During these interviews, a number of helpful insights emerged.

FACTORS THAT AFFECTED ASHLEY'S SUCCESS

From direct observations and interviews with Ashley's teachers and mother, a number of factors that affected the success of Ashley's interactions were identified. In the remainder of this chapter, these factors are discussed and guidelines for improving the quantity and quality of blind and visually impaired children's interactions with peers are proposed.

Ashley's Interactions with Peers

A number of events were observed in the preschool programs. During the first weeks of observation, Ashley engaged in little conversation and play with other children at either program. Her integration was a particular problem at the Sunshine Program, where she was observed in the presence of children who actively engaged classmates in dyadic and group conversation and play, while she was involved with adults—sometimes the classroom teachers, but most often her aide. On a good day, Ashley participated in only a handful of peer interactions, each lasting a short time.

At the BCP, Ashley's interactions with two of her classmates— the two older boys—were restricted primarily to sound play during snack time. During these interactions, the children attended mainly to each other's language, but only minimally to the events and objects in their surroundings. By playing with sounds, the children could easily monitor and respond to each other's interests.

At the Sunshine Program, Ashley also used sound-play games to interact with classmates. While swinging (her favorite outdoor activity) or waiting her turn at the swings, she often engaged in sound play or fantasy conversations with her classmates. I initially thought that swinging provided few benefits to Ashley, but later discovered that it reduced the impact of her blindness during interactions with classmates, which were the longest while she was swinging. During swinging, the boundaries of the activity were limited, and the children's conversations often focused on previous experiences, rather than on current events Ashley could not see. While Ashley's classmates were on the swings, they continued to monitor other children's activities in the playground and sometimes jumped off the swings to join the others. On those occasions, Ashley was left behind without a word of warning to signal her classmates' departures.

Deficits in Ashley's Social Skills

At the start of the field study, I looked for the presence of behaviors that are typical of blind and visually impaired children and would impede interactions between Ashley and her classmates, such as shifting from one topic to another, asking repetitive questions, focusing on their own interests, and failing to respond to and imitate other children's language and behavior. It was not until later that I discovered the impact of the absence of certain behaviors on Ashley's relationships with her classmates and teachers.

Failure to Display Affection

During observations in the classroom, Ashley displayed no affection or attachment to her classmates. This omission first came to light during an interview with Ashley's aide, who said:

> I don't think she has gravitated or warmed up to me in an overly demonstrative way. Sometimes I question, "Shouldn't she be more attached to me? Shouldn't she be more delighted?" If she had been more attached to me, I would, in turn, perhaps feel a greater commitment. I don't think I have had as strong a commitment as I could have if the child were more receptive to me, if we had clicked more. I don't think she dislikes me, but I don't think there's a strong bond. (Kekelis, 1986b, interview on June 11, 1986)

Following the interview with Ashley's aide, a review of field notes indicated that there was no record of Ashley's showing her preference either verbally or nonverbally for any adult or classmate at her preschools. Ashley did not ask about any of her classmates, request to sit beside anyone during snacks or circle time, or reciprocate the positive feelings demonstrated by her classmates. Ashley's aide reflected:

> It's as if she's happy to talk to whoever is there or interact with whoever is there with a few comments or questions. But it's not like she says, "Where's Mary today?" I'm not getting a great many strokes from her, and I think the children would perhaps have been more willing to interact with her if they felt that she at least asked for them. If you don't show them in ways that you're able to show them that you like them, they're not going to be there. (Kekelis, 1986b, interview on June 11, 1986)

In contrast, Ashley's classmates reinforced one another in a number of ways. They smiled and called to their friends at the start of each school day, showed and admired each other's new toys and clothes, and invited each other to birthday parties and overnight parties. Throughout the day, they paid each other compliments and requested and provided assistance to one another.

Unresponsiveness to Classmates

Given the little reinforcement Ashley gave her classmates, it is surprising that some of them repeatedly approached her. Three classmates at the Sunshine Program (Hannah, Nina, and Hilary) showed considerable interest in her. They initiated conversations with her, saved places in line and at the snack table for her, played next to her, and invited her to their homes. Ashley's aide attributed the success of these relationships to the chemistry between the children, but interest in the relationships appeared to be one-sided, since Ashley displayed no preference for any of them.

Although Ashley and these girls seemed to need help in developing a relationship, finding the right way to assist the girls was not easy, as the following example illustrates. One morning Hannah joined Ashley and her aide as they played with blocks and a dollhouse. Ashley played with dolls and furniture on the shelves where they were stored, while Hannah played on the floor. Hoping that the girls' parallel play might develop into a cooperative venture if they sat side by side, I suggested that Ashley play on the floor. Ashley refused to move. She often played with toys on the shelves, rather than on the floor as her classmates did. Ashley's strategy was adaptive for a blind child in a roomful of sighted classmates. With her toys on shelves and her back to other children, she could play without interruption. When her toys were available to classmates, Ashley was vulnerable; other children might step on them, move them, or take them away. Without vision, it was difficult for her to keep track of her possessions and, if necessary, to retrieve them.

On the last day of school, Hannah announced that she had something she wanted to say to Ashley. At the time, Ashley was looking for a misplaced toy and did not respond to her. With the encouragement of her teacher, Hannah extended an invitation for Ashley to visit her during the summer. Ashley did not acknowledge the invitation; at that moment, her attention was focused on her misplaced toy.

The relationship between Ashley and Nina appeared promising at the start of the year, but it never fully developed. While making challah bread for a Shabbat (Sabbath) celebration, Nina announced that she liked Ashley. Recognizing Nina's interest in Ashley, the classroom teachers often asked Nina to take Ashley's hand and guide her to new activities. The two children also engaged in several play episodes when an adult caregiver was not present. During these interactions with Nina, Ashley was exposed to strategies for resolving conflicts, displaying preferences, and making jokes.

Although Ashley's teachers and aide were aware of Nina's interest in Ashley, they did not tell Ashley or encourage her to do or say anything that would have reinforced Nina's interests in her. Before snacks or story time, Nina often told other classmates that she was saving a place for Ashley.

Unfortunately, Ashley was not aware of Nina's intentions and was often guided to a different place by her aide. What was interesting about these unsuccessful attempts was that Nina did not tell Ashley directly that she wanted Ashley to sit by her side.

Need for Prompts by the Aide

Ashley's aide sometimes tried to sustain interactions between Ashley and Nina, but these attempts were not always successful. One morning, the aide suggested that Ashley and Nina try a different activity, since they had been playing by a row of tires and a climbing structure for awhile. Nina walked to a nearby slide and waited for Ashley. When Ashley did not follow her, the aide said, "Ashley, you know what? Nina is waiting for you by the slide." When Ashley failed to move toward the slide, Nina called her, but she did not respond. Her aide commented, "Ashley, Nina is calling you." Then a classroom teacher approached the group and told Nina, "If you want Ashley, maybe you should walk over to her." Nina then returned to the row of tires.

Although Ashley sometimes needed the aide, the children might have worked out conflicts better on their own. For example, Nina may not have gone to the slide without Ashley if Ashley's aide were not present. Perhaps Ashley would not have stayed by the row of tires if her aide were not there and if Nina had not returned to the tires.

On other occasions, Ashley's aide facilitated positive interactions between the two girls. For instance, while the girls were swinging side by side, the aide suggested to Ashley, "Do you want to do a tummy swing? Nina's doing a tummy swing." Ashley proceeded to lie across the swing on her stomach as her friend was doing. This suggestion prompted Ashley to imitate a classmate.

Most of the day, Nina had been attentive to Ashley, responding to and imitating Ashley's actions.

Rejection by a Classmate

The most aggressive attempt to promote a friendship between Ashley and a classmate was made by the mother of one of the students (Sandy) at the Sunshine Program. Unfortunately, the attempt was unsuccessful, perhaps because it was based on the mother's interests, rather than her child's. During Ashley's first month at the preschool, Sandy invited her to lunch. The invitation was probably Sandy's mother's idea, given that Sandy had never interacted with Ashley at school. At the next morning circle, Mrs. Addison asked Sandy's mother if Sandy would sit next to Ashley. Sandy's mother willingly consented, but Sandy was less enthusiastic and agreed only to sit on her mother's lap next to Ashley. For the remainder of the school year, Sandy stayed away from Ashley.

During my final visit to the Sunshine Program, Sandy approached Ashley, but the exchange was disconcerting. Ashley was playing with blocks and dolls. The aide suggested that Sandy build a tunnel alongside Ashley, and Ashley invited Sandy to play with her. Sandy ignored Ashley and her questions and talked only to Ashley's aide. Then, while Sandy was building a house with blocks, Ashley asked her aide to make her house like Sandy's. The interaction continued:

> Aide: (*looking at Sandy*) You want yours like Sandy's. You're neighbors.
> Ashley: Where's Sandy? What's she doing? What are you doing, Sandy?
> Aide: Aren't you going to tell her?
> Sandy: I'm not going to tell her.

At cleanup time, Sandy refused to put away toys near Ashley but tried to help another classmate put away her toys. The attempts to foster a friendship between Sandy and Ashley throughout the school year never succeeded. Perhaps the pressure from her mother to become acquainted with Ashley had been too threatening for Sandy.

WHAT BLINDNESS MEANT TO ASHLEY'S CLASSMATES

There were frequent discussions about Ashley's blindness at the Sunshine Program. When the teachers talked with the students about blindness, they emphasized the things Ashley could do. They also discussed her special needs, which the students learned to accommodate. The children's understanding of Ashley's impairment developed over the months. They learned how Ashley used tactile and auditory cues instead of visual cues to learn about the world and were intrigued with the braille system that Ashley was learning at the BCP, often feeling the braille words.

The children used auditory and tactile cues to help Ashley understand what was going on around her. When Ashley approached the bathroom sink, Nina tapped on the step to signal Ashley to step up. While Hilary made dough for challah, she said to Ashley, "I'm making some for you," and touched Ashley's hand to let Ashley know she was being included.

Ashley did not always welcome nonverbal cues, however. In the following exchange, Ashley seemed to mistake Nina's intentions:

> Nina: (*touching Ashley's shirt*) I'm Nina.
> Ashley: Don't unbutton my shirt.

Ashley's own use of nonverbal contact was also difficult for some of her classmates:

> Ashley: (*approaching Andrea*)
> Andrea: (*to the teacher*) I don't want her touching me.
> Teacher: Tell her.
> Andrea: I don't want you touching me.

Sometimes the children's use of nonverbal behaviors revealed that they did not understand fully what it means to be blind. The children pointed toward objects, held out toys, and nodded to Ashley. Unless an adult was present to put their actions into words, Ashley was unaware of these nonverbal messages. Ashley's language and actions may have made it difficult for her classmates to understand that she could not see. Although Ashley was totally blind, she often appeared to be sighted, since her eyes were not disfigured and she oriented toward her partners and used gestures, such as pointing and offering objects. She also used the words look and see, which sometimes led to misunderstandings with her classmates:

> Donovan: (*approaching Ashley with a handful of jelly beans*)
> Ashley: Can I see?
> Donovan: (*putting jelly beans near Ashley's eyes*)
> Teacher: You have to put them by her hands because she sees with her hands.

Ashley and her classmates at the Sunshine Program often engaged in indirect interactions. Perhaps if her aide had not been so readily available, the children would have talked directly to one another. In the following exchange, Ashley and Melody were doing artwork at the same table inside the classroom while their classmates were outside:

Ashley:　Why is Melody staying inside?
Aide:　Ask her.
Ashley:　Why is Melody staying inside?
Melody:　Because I want to draw.

Inside the playhouse, Ashley was setting a table while her aide watched. Hannah came over and watched Ashley.

Aide:　Hi Hannah.
Hannah:　What is Ashley doing?
Aide:　You can ask her.
Hannah:　You.
Ashley:　I'm pouring coffee. You can't really have it. It's yucky.

EVALUATING PEER INTERACTIONS

Ashley's caregivers evaluated her interactions with peers on the basis of their expectations for Ashley's mainstreaming experience and the norms they used to evaluate Ashley's behavior. Both of these factors are discussed in the following section.

Expectations for Ashley's Preschool Experiences

Ashley was competent in her conversations with adults. She listened to their questions and comments, responded with appropriate language, asked for explanations when unable to follow their conversations, and creatively expanded on their ideas. She actively engaged adults in interactions and seemed to prefer their company to that of peers. She needed to develop skills that were important for peer interactions—skills that she could not master during interactions with her mother and teachers. To develop these skills, Ashley needed opportunities to interact with her classmates at both preschools.

The teachers at the Sunshine Program had two motives for wanting Ashley in their program. They wanted to learn more about blindness and they wanted their students exposed to individuals with special needs to teach them to be responsible and to help their friends.

The staff at the BCP focused on Ashley's needs. They taught her to follow instructions, to respect adult authority, and to make transitions. Although they recognized the importance of peer interactions, there was no appropriate partner for Ashley in the program. The instructor of the BCP had been willing to initiate a reverse mainstreaming program by bringing in nondisabled children of Ashley's age, but the Addisons chose to place Ashley in the Sunshine Program.

The staff at both preschools made sporadic attempts to foster interactions between Ashley and her classmates. They encouraged classmates to take Ashley's hand and lead her to an activity and informed Ashley of the location of her classmates. However, these efforts were not sufficient to increase significantly the number of interactions between Ashley and her peers.

Norms for Ashley: Involvement with Peers

It is often difficult for both families and professionals to establish appropriate expectations for a disabled child. They frequently consider whatever a disabled child does to be exceptional. For Ashley and other disabled children who have the potential to be highly competent, inappropriate expectations may limit their achievements.

When I compared Ashley with her sighted classmates at the Sunshine Program, she appeared to be developmentally delayed. She engaged in few interactions with peers, but she often talked with adults; she engaged in too little group play and too much solitary play; she played too long at her favorite activities, but she played too briefly with peers; and she made few attempts to display her interest in and preference for any of her classmates. Staff at the Sunshine Program did not seem to be particularly concerned with the disparity between the social experiences of Ashley and the other children in the classroom.

CONSTRUCTING EXPECTATIONS FOR ASHLEY

The teachers and aide at the Sunshine Program did not receive adequate pre- or in-service training to prepare them for working with a blind child. It was their first opportunity to work with a disabled child, and it was difficult for them to construct appropriate expectations for Ashley.

On several occasions, the staff discussed the importance of treating Ashley as they treated her classmates, yet the way in which they spoke to her reflected their ambivalent feelings toward her. For example, they used language that was similar to the language used with infants (Snow & Ferguson, 1977). When speaking to Ashley, they used proper names instead of pronouns, spoke in a high pitch and exaggerated their intonation, asked many questions, and often used baby-talk words. During an interview, the head instructor described Ashley as remarkable and more advanced and stronger than her classmates, yet she spoke to Ashley as she would to a toddler.

The instructors also had difficulty disciplining Ashley. One teacher recounted: "We kind of had a fight, Ashley and I. I'd say to myself, 'Oh no,' because there's this image I have that Ashley loves me. That was hard." (Kekelis, 1986b, interview on June 24, 1986). Although this instructor may have wanted to be liked by all her students, she was swifter to set limits for the others and did less to avoid confrontations with the sighted students than with Ashley. For example, one morning, when the tables were covered with shaving cream that the children used to create sculptures, Ashley repeatedly spread her hands across the table and into her classmates' work. Despite frequent warnings from her classmates to stop, she continued to encroach on their play areas, and she greatly agitated her classmates. Observing the problem, the classroom teacher explained to the children that Ashley could not see where her space ended and theirs began. However, it seemed to me that Ashley was intentionally provoking her classmates. The conflict continued, and the instructor threatened to remove Ashley from the activity table, but she did not. Instead, she moved Ashley to another side of the table after it was vacated. If another child had acted as Ashley did, the child would have been removed immediately from the table and made to sit on a chair during time-out.

Even when the staff attempted to encourage Ashley to behave as her classmates did, they were not always successful. Ashley had difficulty making transitions from one activity and setting to another. She not only walked slowly, but she liked to stop along the routes to explore and talk about objects. Getting from one place to another was not a means to an end but an end in itself. As a result, Ashley was frequently out of sync with her classmates. She began activities after children had found partners and continued them long after her classmates had moved on to new tasks.

The staff and I developed a plan to help Ashley keep up with her classmates. Five minutes before transitions, Ashley's aide encouraged her to proceed to a new setting. The extra time enabled Ashley to participate in more activities with classmates, but the intervention was not entirely successful.

For a few weeks, Ashley refused to follow her teachers' instructions. For example, when it was time to wash up before snack time, she refused to stop the activity in which she was engaged. When given the option of obeying the rules or missing snacks, she chose to miss snacks and sit by herself while her classmates ate. On one occasion, she chose not to participate in a classmate's birthday party. (No other child in the class ever chose to miss snack time or a birthday party.)

When other students were removed from a group's activities for a few minutes because of their misconduct, they watched their classmates' activities and appeared upset not to be part of their peer group. In contrast, Ashley displayed no signs of dissatisfaction when she was unable to participate in snacks, religious ceremonies, or birthday festivities. During class time, she was not involved in peer activities to the same extent as were her classmates, and since Ashley could not see what she was missing, time-outs did not encourage her to behave more like her classmates.

INTERACTIONS WITH SUBSTITUTE TEACHERS

On several occasions, Ashley's aide was unable to supervise her at the Sunshine Program, and substitute caregivers from within the preschool were provided. These occasions presented opportunities to observe interactions between Ashley and persons who were inexperienced in working with blind or visually impaired children.

The first substitute, Emily, engaged in constant conversation with Ashley. As a result, Ashley had no need to look to her classmates for attention and partnership, and her classmates had no opportunity to play or talk with Ashley. During the morning, Ashley broke a plastic fork while playing with clay. Observing the accident, one of Ashley's classmates found a replacement. She offered the fork to Emily and said, "Here's another for her." Emily was a go-between. Later, during snack time, the classroom teacher asked one of the children to pass a can of juice to another child. When the boy asked to whom he should pass the juice, Ashley announced that she wanted the juice. Unfortunately, Emily had anticipated Ashley's needs and had already served her juice.

A few weeks later, when one of the classroom teachers was absent, a substitute teacher, Jill, filled in. Jill also engaged in long conversations with Ashley that interfered with Ashley's participation in class activities. On a number of occasions, Jill talked to Ashley through her aide. At the start of the school day, Jill came up to Ashley and her aide and inquired, "How has Ashley been this morning? Is she enjoying herself?" Ashley's aide instructed Jill to talk directly to Ashley.

FACTORS AFFECTING POSITIVE PEER INTERACTIONS

During the months of observation of Ashley and her classmates in both preschools, the following factors were found to affect Ashley's preschool experience:

- *Preservice and in-service training of teachers.* The staff at the Sunshine Program had never worked with a blind or visually impaired child and were uncertain of the goals and teaching approach to adopt with Ashley. It would have been helpful for them to have talked with the counselor who had worked with Ashley and her family during the previous three years. The counselor knew Ashley's strengths and weaknesses and may have been able to suggest ways to help Ashley become a more active participant in the program.

- *Priorities for Ashley's mainstreaming experience.* The staff at the Sunshine Program did not have a definite set of priorities for mainstreaming Ashley. Much of what they did limited the interactions between Ashley and her classmates because they did not realize the importance of these interactions.

- *Attempts to monitor Ashley's progress.* There was no systematic attempt to monitor Ashley's progress in the Sunshine Program. Short weekly meetings in which staff could discuss factors that had appeared to promote or impede positive social experiences should have been scheduled. Information gathered during these meetings could then have been used for the systematic design of activities, settings, and play groups that might stimulate peer interactions.

- *Communication with staff at both programs.* Although the instructors at Ashley's preschools were interested in each others' work, they never met. It would have been informative for the staff members of both programs to have observed Ashley in another setting and to maintain regular telephone contact. Ashley's instructors at the BCP could have helped the staff at the Sunshine Program develop more demanding expectations for Ashley. In addition, through such contacts, the staffs could have developed a preschool experience with continuity for Ashley.

- *Communication within the programs.* Staff at the Sunshine Program had opinions of each other's work that they did not openly discuss. By sharing their different perspectives, they could have improved their efforts to mainstream Ashley.

- *Less adult supervision of Ashley.* During much of her time at the Sunshine Program, Ashley was in safe situations in which she did not require constant supervision by adults. Perhaps Ashley's aide could have remained near enough to monitor Ashley and her peers but far enough away not to regulate them. If Ashley was alone more frequently at the Sunshine Program, she might have been more motivated to initiate interactions with her classmates.

- *Creation of a safe and predictable environment.* A classroom of 20 active children can be disconcerting for a totally blind child. No wonder Ashley was protective of her play area and materials. If play space had been arranged for Ashley in the corners of the room or in the loft away from the hustle of her classmates, Ashley might have found it easier to play with one or two classmates. Such an area could have been marked off with furniture or blocks and restricted to Ashley and one or two friends.

- *Reinforcement of interactions between Ashley and her classmates.* Ashley was often reinforced by adults when she was *not* interacting with classmates. Ashley may have approached her classmates more often if her caregivers had attended to and reinforced her when she was with peers rather than by herself. It would also have been helpful to model ways for Ashley to show her classmates that she wanted to be their friend. Interactions among young children present important opportunities to acquire language and social skills. For sighted children, these interactions require the minimal involvement of adults. For blind and visually impaired children, however, they require thoughtful planning and monitoring by classroom teachers and aides.

Chapter 4

The Effects of Visual Impairment on Children's Social Interactions in Regular Education Programs

Linda S. Kekelis and Sharon Zell Sacks

The goals of the study that will be reported in this chapter were to collect descriptive information on the social interactions of blind and visually impaired children in school settings and to recommend strategies that could enhance the children's development of social skills and maximize their integration into educational mainstream settings. Six children were observed in the study, and the following criteria were used to select them:

1. Visual impairment meeting the legal definition of blindness (20/200 visual acuity or less in the better eye with best correction or a visual field restriction of 20 degrees or less).

2. Enrollment in an integrated kindergarten or first-grade class.

3. Overall good health and no additional disabilities.

With the assistance of the Blind Babies Foundation, a home-based program that serves approximately 300 families in the San Francisco Bay area, and the aid of special education teachers in nearby school districts, we identified prospective children for the study. Table 1 presents information on the ages, diagnoses, visual impairments, and levels of participation of the six children who were chosen.

Table 1. Description of Children by Age, Diagnosis, Visual
Impairment, and Participation in Regular Education Classroom

Child	Age	Diagnosis	Degree of Visual Impairment	Participation in Regular Education
Bruce	5	Macular degeneration	Legally blind[1]	Fully mainstreamed in kindergarten
Lee	6	Complications from chicken pox	Has minimal light perception	Fully mainstreamed in kindergarten
Nicole	6	Bilateral rod and cone dysfunction	Legally blind	Fully mainstreamed in kindergarten–first grade
Tom	6	Retinopathy of prematurity	Has light perception	Partially mainstreamed in kindergarten with a classroom aide for half the school day
Jena	7	Retinopathy of prematurity	Totally blind	Partially mainstreamed in kindergarten with a classroom aide for half the school day
Karen	8	Corneal dystrophy	Legally blind	Partially mainstreamed in a first-grade class 40 percent of the school day

[1]Near the end of the study, the degree of Bruce's vision loss was determined to be less severe than had been thought.

We chose to study only a few children so we could carefully document the development of relationships and the patterns of interaction between the visually impaired children and their sighted classmates and identify factors that affected the integration of the visually impaired students into regular education classrooms. Analyses of this nature are time consuming, but they provide important information about developmental processes and environmental factors that contribute to the optimal development of blind and visually impaired students. On the basis of such in-depth studies, we have generated hypotheses regarding the development of the children, which can be tested in experimental studies with larger groups of children.

RESEARCH METHOD

The majority of studies of children's social skills have had limited generalizability because of their methodological weaknesses. This study was designed to eliminate some of these problems. In the following discussion, issues that relate to the study's methodology are examined.

Formation of Relationships

In most studies in this area, classmates' interactions are examined long after the social order of classrooms has been established. Although this approach may identify children who require intervention, it does not identify factors, including social behaviors and physical appearance, that may be responsible for the social isolation of these children. Thus, most studies cannot determine whether children's social behaviors are the cause of their social standing among peers or the result of being liked or disliked by classmates (Moore, 1967).

We began our classroom observations right after the visually impaired children entered their kindergarten and first-grade classes. By documenting the development of social relationships and interactions among classmates for an entire school year, we identified specific factors that affected the children's status among their classmates.

Structured Activities and Unstructured Free Play

Each child was observed once a week for an entire morning or afternoon session. During these visits, which lasted for several hours, we observed social interactions in a variety of contexts: during peer-directed activities (such as playing house or Simon Says) in the classrooms and on playgrounds and during teacher-directed activities (such as listening to stories and participating in show-and-tell) in the classrooms.

Each set of activities—peer directed and teacher directed—placed unique demands on the visually impaired children. The children's display of competence and their acceptance by classmates in one set of activities did not ensure their success in others. Only by observing peer- and teacher-directed activities in both classrooms and on playgrounds were we able to gain a complete understanding of these children's social interactions in mainstream programs.

Longitudinal Data

By observing the children over most of the school year, we were able to determine elements of their social lives at school that remained constant, as well as those that changed. For example, in one classroom, seat assignments were changed several times during the year. Being present for each of these changes made it possible to examine a number of concerns: the attitudes and behaviors of classmates toward the visually impaired child; fluctuations in the visually impaired child's behavior, depending on his or her seat assignment; and changes in the classroom teacher's support for the visually impaired child following each seat assignment.

The longitudinal study also yielded a number of serendipitous findings that arose from observations of infrequent events in the classroom that were nevertheless critical for understanding the children's social needs. For example, after several weeks of appropriate behavior in the classroom, one visually impaired student's level of competence plunged dramatically when his kindergarten class was taught by a substitute teacher. This student was affected by the change to a significantly greater extent than were his sighted classmates, who were able to manage without their teacher's guidance and support for a brief time.

Ethnographic Approach

Ethnographic studies attempt to describe social interactions of communities by understanding the meaning of life's experiences from an insider's perspective. To achieve this goal, ethnographers adopt a more open-ended approach to data collection and analysis than is used in most social science studies. Although we began the study with a number of concerns and hypotheses that were based on our previous work with blind and visually impaired children, we did not restrict our investigation to these concerns. As Agar (1980, p. 71) pointed out, "ethnography is the more general process of understanding another human group; hypothesis-testing is a minor, though potentially significant part of that process."

By using an ethnographic approach, we were able to identify issues of importance to visually impaired children, rather than base our analyses on previous work with nondisabled children. We used the data collected on the visually impaired children who participated in the project to generate our research concerns.

Although all research methods affect the social interactions that are studied, ethnography tries to minimize the interference of observational methods (Dobbert, 1982). We tried to be as unobtrusive as possible so as not to disrupt everyday classroom routines. We quietly observed the visually impaired children and their classmates, made field notes, and participated in conversations and activities when it seemed appropriate. At times, we filled in for classroom aides, participated in holiday celebrations, and helped the children with academic lessons, because we were aware that total uninvolvement would have interfered with the naturalness of ongoing interactions (Schatzman & Strauss, 1973; Spradley, 1980).

Data Collection

During observations, we took field notes that described classroom activities, recorded conversations between the visually impaired children and their classmates, and recorded comments by teachers and classmates regarding the visually impaired students. After each observation, we rewrote and expanded the field notes. The expanded accounts included *observational notes*, which described the who, what, when, and how of events; *theoretical notes*, which interpreted events and generated hypotheses for future study; and *methodological notes*, which addressed methodological problems and suggested new observational approaches for subsequent visits. Each day's notes took several hours to rewrite. The rewriting of these notes provided direction for future observations and allowed us to deal reflect upon the experiences of observing and participating in each classroom.

Interviews with Teachers

We obtained information on the mainstreaming of the visually impaired students from classroom and resource-room teachers at periodic intervals throughout the project. Both formal interviews, in which the teachers were asked a standard set of questions, and informal interviews, in which inquiries were tailored to the unique concerns of each classroom, were conducted. These discussions provided an opportunity to obtain information on the children's family lives and medical histories, to learn about significant events that took place during our absences, and to discover the motivation for the teachers' involvement or, at times, uninvolvement in the mainstreaming of the visually impaired children in their classrooms.

Interviews with Children

During the last two months of the study, we conducted formal interviews with the visually impaired children and their sighted classmates. Each student was asked individually the following set of questions:

- Who are your best friends in the class?
- Why do you like them?
- Now, I want you to think if there are some children you don't like. Don't tell me their names. Why don't you like them?
- When your teacher chooses partners for you to play with during free-play time, who do you like to play with?
- When your teacher chooses partners for lessons, who do you like to work with?
- Do you ever play with _____ [the visually impaired classmate]?
- What kinds of things can you do together?
- What can't you two play?
- What does it mean to be blind or visually impaired?

These interviews provided sociometric data that we used to ascertain the degree to which the visually impaired children were accepted by classmates both as playmates and workmates. In addition, they provided insights into the dynamics of the entire social network of the five classrooms.

We also talked with the children to understand their perspectives of the events we witnessed during visits. These informal discussions helped explain the motivation of both amicable and antisocial behaviors displayed by the visually impaired children and their sighted classmates.

CASE STUDIES

Case studies of three of the visually impaired children who participated in the field study are presented in the following discussion to illustrate the complexity of mainstreaming visually impaired children in classrooms with sighted classmates. The case studies of Lee, Bruce, and Nicole reveal the relationship between a visually impaired student's special needs, the classroom milieu, and the participation of teachers in the regular classroom and resource room. The factors associated with successful and unsuccessful mainstreaming are discussed after the presentation of the case studies.

Lee

Lee, who was 6 years old during the study, was a Vietnamese child who moved with his family to the United States when he was 3 years old. After contracting chicken pox at 8 months, he was left with minimal light perception. When he entered a preschool program for visually impaired children at age 4, he knew only a few English words. In 1 1/2 years, however, he had considerably mastered English. With early intervention, Lee acquired communicative as well as social and cognitive skills that were age appropriate. During the field study, he continued to attend the special program for visually impaired children in the morning and the kindergarten class with sighted children in the afternoon.

Social Skills

Although Lee's visual impairment was severe, he participated in classroom activities and in conversations with classmates to a greater extent than did four of the other children in the field study. His personality and social skills, along with the classroom environment and classroom teacher's ability to adapt her teaching style to meet the needs of a visually impaired student, played a role in his integration into the classroom. The experiences he had at home and the expectations of his family may have played an important role in his socialization at school.

Lee's ability to initiate interactions and to display his preference for classmates (through expressions of his feelings for favorite classmates and requests for their company when working on academic tasks) made him a child who was easy for children and adults to like. Unlike many blind and visually impaired children, whose speech is self-centered, Lee frequently introduced topics that addressed the actions and feelings of others. He showed interest in the actions and possessions of classmates and often asked appropriate questions about their interests during class discussions.

In addition to his verbal skills, Lee possessed exceptional orientation and mobility abilities for a visually impaired child. He knew his way around the classroom and the playground and moved to his destinations with considerable speed. When students were assigned to help him on trips to the auditorium or library, his mobility skills made it relatively easy for them to keep up with classmates. In fact, Lee and his partner often led the class and set a brisk pace for the other students.

Influence of the Classroom Teacher

At the start of the school year, the students varied in their willingness to interact with Lee. We overheard comments by some classmates that they did not wish to sit near Lee. These attitudes could have affected Lee's opportunities to learn from classmates if his teacher had not intervened.

Students in Lee's class were assigned seats during a number of activities, and these seat assignments were changed several times during the year. The seating arrangement placed boys and girls side by side. In the classrooms where children were allowed to choose their own seats, classmates rarely sat with children of the opposite sex and were less likely to develop relationships with classmates of the opposite sex. By changing the seating at regular intervals, Lee's teacher encouraged the children to become acquainted with a variety of classmates, including those of the opposite sex. The seat assignments were especially important for Lee, since they helped him get to know several classmates—those who sat next to him as well as the friends of classmates who sat near him. It was with these children that Lee formed friendships. In one instance, a classmate who had initially expressed displeasure in having Lee as a neighbor grew to enjoy his company and participated in conversations with him throughout the year.

In selecting children to sit near Lee, the kindergarten teacher considered those who displayed an interest in Lee and those who were socially skilled and well liked by their peers. During much of the school year, Lee was seated near the boy and girl who were most popular. These children were academically and socially skilled and frequently interacted with Lee both in the classroom and on the playground. Being in the company of these popular students also brought Lee into contact with other classmates who were socially skilled.

The classroom teacher's attempts to improve Lee's academic skills also helped Lee become an integral member of the class. At the start of the year, Lee had difficulty attending to class discussions and engaged in self-stimulatory behavior that disrupted classmates. To reduce these behaviors, the teacher found ways to increase Lee's interest in the class discussions.

For example, Lee sat next to the teacher during circle time, so he could explore the objects and toys discussed during academic lessons and show-and-tell tactilely. Frequently, the teacher gave him objects to hold during discussions to retain his interest and to improve his understanding of the verbal information being provided. For example, during a discussion of grapes and wine making, Lee was given some grape vines to hold. While his classmates maintained visual contact with the topic of conversation, ⌐ maintained physical contact with the topic and stayed focused on the discussion. When Lee had nothing to hold his attention, he sometimes lost interest and disturbed classmates or lay down on the floor.

During activities and discussions in which each student was given a turn to respond, the teacher often called on Lee first or early in the activity. This approach helped capture Lee's interest and reduced the likelihood of his tuning out. On those occasions when Lee's attention wandered, the teacher called on him before he began disrupting other classmates.

When new concepts were presented to the class, Lee was frequently called upon to help the teacher illustrate the new material to the other students. To help Lee understand these concepts, the teacher appealed to all the senses of her students. Both Lee's and his classmates' understanding of the concepts was increased by this approach. Lee was also presented as the model of appropriate behavior from which his classmates learned, which enhanced his role in the class. While he required the help of classmates in some circumstances, Lee was also the one who was frequently chosen by his teacher to demonstrate new skills.

The importance of these strategies came to light when Lee's kindergarten teacher was absent and substitute teachers instructed the class. The two substitute teachers made no effort to adapt their instructional methods for Lee. Their lessons were visually oriented, they did not explain activities adequately, and they called on Lee to participate after considerable waiting periods. By the time Lee was called on, he had disturbed classmates sitting near him and was unable to provide the appropriate responses the teachers requested. On those occasions, the classmates criticized his inappropriate behavior and engaged in less positive interactions with him in the classroom and on the playground. Furthermore, Lee's degree of discomfort in these situations was apparent from his requests to leave the classroom and return to his special preschool classroom.

Intervention of the Special Education Teacher

Because Lee's presence in the kindergarten increased the workload of the classroom teacher, the special education teacher tried to lessen some of the classroom teacher's responsibilities by becoming actively involved in the kindergarten class. Each day, she instructed Lee in the use of braille in the classroom and modified materials so Lee could participate in activities. By spending time in the kindergarten rather than taking Lee out of the classroom, she facilitated a number of positive interactions between Lee and his classmates. She was adept at providing assistance without overwhelming the children, so the interactions remained child directed rather than teacher directed.

The special education teacher gave the children as much information about Lee's visual impairment as they needed or were interested in hearing at a particular time and repeated certain facts when necessary. On several occasions, we observed children trying to help Lee find his seat in the classroom or locate a classmate on the playground by using gestures. They also forgot correct techniques for guiding Lee in the classroom and the hallways. When the special education teacher observed these problems, she reminded the children how to guide Lee in a safe manner.

Effects of Visual Impairment

Despite Lee's achievements and acceptance by his classmates, his visual impairment significantly affected the kinds of interactions in which he and his classmates participated. After greeting one another, Lee and his classmates found it difficult to maintain conversations and play. They wanted to interact with one another, but Lee's visual impairment made it difficult for them to know what to do together. Most of the interactions among the kindergartners were stimulated and maintained by the visual perceptions they shared.

The impact of Lee's visual impairment was particularly evident during free play in the playground. For example, Lee's classmates enjoyed calling out to Lee and encouraged him to chase them around the playground. For several months, he did so, but one day he revealed his true feelings about the game in an unexpected outburst of emotion. Several of Lee's classmates repeatedly approached Lee and called out his name, but each time Lee came toward them, the classmates ran away. Later, the children returned and greeted Lee several times before he responded. When he did answer their greetings, he shouted for them to get away. The classmates were upset by Lee's reaction, but they did not attempt to talk with him about the problem. When we asked Lee what was wrong, he explained that the classmates had hurt his feelings because they repeatedly ran away and left him behind. When the classmates heard this comment, they promised not to abandon Lee and kept their promises. Although these children's intentions had never been malicious, they were not able to develop a more positive way to interact with Lee during recess time.

The case study of Lee revealed that with support from a classroom teacher who adequately addressed the social needs of her students and with in-class assistance from a special education teacher, a blind child can have opportunities to interact with classmates and be well liked by classmates. However, Lee's visual impairment did have a profound influence on the quality of these interactions, especially on children's ability to maintain play interactions for any length of time and to engage in conversations about a variety of topics.

Bruce

Bruce was 5 years old during the field study. His vision loss, the result of macular degeneration, was initially reported to result in a visual acuity of 20/200, but we learned later that his vision loss was less severe. Although Bruce's visual impairment was the least severe of the six children we observed, it significantly affected his ability to carry out academic assignments and to engage in play with peers. Bruce's social deficits, the insufficient classroom-management skills of the kindergarten teacher, and the resource-room teacher's lack of involvement in his education outside the resource room resulted in an isolating mainstream experience. Bruce's kindergarten experience illustrates the special needs of visually impaired students who may sometimes appear to be unimpaired but who nevertheless require considerable assistance to participate in positive social exchanges with classmates.

Social Skills

Bruce engaged in solitary play or wandered around the classroom observing the activities of other students. Early in the school year, he did not attempt to engage in play or conversations with classmates. Late in the school year, the exchanges he initiated were negative and provoked classmates to attack him verbally and physically.

Despite Bruce's lack of social skills or motivation to interact with classmates, the kindergarten teacher did not intervene to reduce his isolation. Rather, on several occasions she praised

Bruce's ability to persist at solitary activities and commented that kindergarten-aged children engage primarily in parallel and solitary play and therefore that she was not concerned about Bruce's behavior. The resource-room teacher attributed the differences in the frequency and quality of Bruce's social interactions with sighted peers to his age, since he was slightly younger than many of his classmates. By not realizing that Bruce's social skills were inadequate, neither the kindergarten teacher nor the resource-room teacher considered it necessary to supervise Bruce carefully or intervene in his exchanges with classmates.

Teacher's Involvement in Promoting Interactions

We witnessed several notable exchanges between Bruce and his classmates in the classroom and on the playground. During the first hour of play in Bruce's classroom, the children often played several board games. Although these games could have been a way for Bruce to become acquainted with classmates and to acquire skills for initiating and maintaining conversations and resolving disagreements, they were the cause of unproductive conflicts. One morning, as Bruce wandered aimlessly around the classroom, the kindergarten teacher asked a classmate if he wanted to play checkers with Bruce. The classmate refused, stating, "He doesn't know how to play." When asked to teach Bruce the game, the classmate said he did not want to. Another classmate was willing to teach Bruce how to play checkers, but he did not know how to communicate the rules of the game in a way that Bruce could understand. Commands such as, "No, you can't move like that," did not clarify what Bruce had done incorrectly or what he needed to do in future moves.

Once, while Bruce played checkers, he made a number of mistakes for which he was severely criticized. His partner grew progressively impatient and finally ended the game. In trying to repair his mistakes, Bruce offered to play a turn over again, but his partner refused. His classmate was upset because he thought that Bruce's mistakes were willful attempts to cheat.

On still another occasion, the kindergarten teacher encouraged Bruce to play a popular board game with three other students. She briefly explained the rules of the game, watched the children take their first turns, and returned periodically to resolve their conflicts. Bruce had considerable problems playing the game and often accidentally moved the game pieces of classmates or moved his game piece in the wrong direction. He made these errors partly because he could not see the board and the game pieces well enough and partly because the chaotic manner in which his classmates played made it difficult for him to follow.

Again, the teacher had selected the wrong children as partners for Bruce. These children had difficulty waiting their turns, shouted and moved about the playing area during the game, and responded angrily to Bruce's mistakes. Several times, they accused Bruce of cheating. When Bruce moved closer to the board to locate his game piece, trying to be more careful during later turns, a classmate yelled, "Get your head back." No one understood that Bruce could not see well. No one offered him assistance.

Bruce required significantly more assistance to learn the rules of the games and to participate in them. If the games had been adapted for Bruce and if his partners had been reminded of his special needs, Bruce may have been able to play them better. Without adequate support, Bruce not only failed at the games, but was perceived as socially incompetent by classmates.

Bruce's kindergarten teacher was present on many occasions when it would have been appropriate to discuss Bruce's visual impairment. One day while the teacher was reading a book to the class, Bruce moved from the back of the room closer to the teacher. A classmate criticized him for changing places, not understanding that Bruce was trying to see the picture book. When the teacher placed the book close to Bruce so he could see the pictures, one child complained, "Don't just hold it up in front of somebody." Another student commented, "She's holding it up in his face." The teacher's only comment to the students was, "I have to do that." It was no wonder that the students displayed little understanding of Bruce's behavior.

Effects of the Classroom Environment
The classroom environment also contributed to Bruce's inability to interact positively with classmates. Each day began with an hour-long period of free play in which students could select their activities, areas of play, and partners. Considerable amounts of play materials and school supplies were available to Bruce and his classmates, but the lack of organization and rules resulted in their misuse. Rather than providing the means for students to play in a cooperative manner, the classroom's toys and materials generated numerous conflicts.

Without rules governing the termination of one activity and the initiation of another, it was common for children in Bruce's class to wander in and out of play areas, disrupting the ongoing interactions of classmates. It was also easy for them to abandon activities when conflicts arose, rather than negotiate compromises with their peers.

Throughout the day, Bruce and his classmates were allowed to select their places. This practice resulted in interactions with a restricted set of classmates, since many chose to spend all their time with the same set of children, and conflicts arose frequently among the cliques that were generated. During visits to Bruce's classroom, it was rare to see boys and girls or children of different races conversing and playing together in a positive manner.

For Bruce, these seating arrangements were particularly deleterious. He generally sat alone during circle time and played by himself during free play. If the teacher had placed Bruce in the company of socially skilled classmates who were willing to show him special consideration, he would have been exposed to peers who modeled appropriate strategies for initiating interactions and resolving conflicts.

Several cliques in Bruce's class disrupted the play and conversations of students inside and outside the classroom. Students from two of the groups frequently engaged in verbal and physical assaults on classmates. The teacher's attention focused on the conflicts created by these groups, rather than on constructive educational activities for all the children.

Bruce's visual impairment had a considerable impact on his social interactions with classmates. Unfortunately, his kindergarten teacher did little to improve his social standing among classmates or to increase his social competence. The few attempts she made failed because she withdrew her support before Bruce was able to participate independently in social exchanges.

Services of the Resource-Room Teacher

The services Bruce received from the resource-room teacher addressed only academic concerns. This teacher did not attempt to improve his social skills or his interactions with classmates. The relationship between Bruce's deficits in social skills; the chaotic and, at times, hostile classroom environment; and the failure of both the classroom and resource-room teachers to intervene resulted in a deleterious mainstreaming experience for Bruce.

Nicole

Nicole, who was 6 years old at the time of the study, was legally blind. Before enrolling in the kindergarten–first-grade classroom, she attended a preschool with nondisabled children. After the morning class, she was instructed each day in a resource room. Nicole had adequate verbal and social skills for a child of her age. Her outgoing personality and interest in her peers helped her gain access to their company.

Influence of the Classroom Teacher

For Nicole, the positive outcomes from mainstreaming were, to a great extent, due to the competence and dedication of her classroom teacher. In our discussions, the teacher said he regarded Nicole much like a sighted child—as Bruce's kindergarten teacher said she regarded Bruce. However, Nicole's teacher addressed the individual differences of each of his students; he took their learning styles and personalities into account when he instructed them and evaluated their work. With Nicole, he expected adherence to the rules of the classroom and reprimanded her when she spoke out of turn or did not follow directions. He also took Nicole's visual impairment into consideration and, at times, provided her with extra support. He set up situations so classmates helped Nicole complete assignments, and he picked students who were competent and had the patience to work with her. As a result, these tutoring experiences could be positive for both Nicole and her classmates.

Nicole's teacher closely attended to both the public and private interactions of the students, so inappropriate behaviors were readily corrected and appropriate behaviors were acknowledged. He helped Nicole and her classmates understand the impact of their actions on each other, suggested ways for them to remain friends, and regularly encouraged them to consider each other's feelings and interests and to assume responsibility for each other's welfare.

Effects of the Classroom Environment

The structure of activities helped create a classroom environment that was stimulating and conducive to positive and extended social interactions. Each morning, the students could choose to play in small groups at stations with various toys and activities. The size of the groups was determined by the toys that were selected. By exercising control over the number of children in each play group, the teacher facilitated conversations and cooperative play among the students and minimized conflicts. During these activities, he supervised students at a distance and was available, when necessary, to provide assistance.

The combination of an orderly classroom environment and a variety of activities that truly interested students benefited all the students. Nicole and her classmates demonstrated regard for each other's welfare, and most of the students' interactions were constructive and enhanced their social competence.

Effects of Visual Impairment

In the early weeks of our observations, Nicole's visual impairment did not seem to affect her interactions with classmates adversely. Later, however, we began to see that certain limitations were imposed by her visual condition with which she had difficulty coping.

In Nicole's class, there were teacher-directed, highly structured activities, along with open-ended activities that allowed students to exercise their creativity. Reading and writing skills and creative arts were practiced daily, and the teacher gave minilectures that covered a wide range of subjects, including space travel, geography, and cooking. This curriculum accentuated the impact of Nicole's visual impairment on her ability to learn and interact with peers. Nicole was able to participate fully in activities that were social, but had considerable difficulty keeping up with her peers academically.

Relationship with Peers

It was difficult for Nicole to accept that classmates did not want to work with her during academic activities. During social activities in the classroom and during recess time, Nicole shared the company of three girls, but she was sometimes left out of this group during academic activities. Observing the effects of this isolation on Nicole, the teacher spoke with the students about Nicole's feelings and helped Nicole understand that friends do not always play and work together. His intercession immediately put an end to the escalation of conflicts in Nicole's peer group and addressed Nicole's feelings of rejection.

There were other instances when classmates would not allow Nicole to participate in the activities she was willing to attempt. During an activity in which students were required to construct model neighborhoods and animal yards, Nicole teamed up with Cindy, a favorite classmate. Throughout the activity, Cindy exercised control over the constructions and rejected all Nicole's suggestions and attempts to help. She made comments such as,

"You're ruining the road. Nicole, Nicole, you're messing up. We can't have a zoo with messed up roads." When Nicole tried to help landscape the zoo, Cindy told her, "You're making all the trees fall. You can't decorate the trees. When you put the trees up, they wiggle." Although Nicole was visibly upset by these comments, she said nothing to defend herself and retreated, providing only minimal help. This approach temporarily appeased Cindy, who said, "I'll give you the trees and you can do it, all right?" Unfortunately, because of her response to Cindy's control, Nicole did not learn the intended goals of the activity.

It may have been the result of such interactions that Nicole developed interactive strategies to increase her acceptance by peers. She tried to direct activities less frequently and solicited the opinions of classmates before suggesting ideas. Thus, she was more likely to say and do what was agreeable to her classmates, and her input was less likely to be rejected. It was important for Nicole to find the means to increase her chances of being accepted by peers, and it was also important for her to be able to assert herself and pursue her interests. Adult supervision was necessary to help Nicole balance these two goals.

Activities of the Resource-Room Teacher

Nicole's resource-room teacher focused on academic skills. For Nicole, this help was adequate because her classroom teacher addressed her social needs.

The resource-room teacher could have improved Nicole's classroom experience if she had helped Nicole deal with difficult, visually oriented tasks, rather than attempt to avoid them. When activities required attending to visual stimuli, Nicole sometimes did little to master them. When the classroom teacher gave directions for these activities, Nicole did not pay attention; instead, she talked with classmates. When an aide or classmate tried to help her complete the tasks, Nicole often refused to cooperate or tried to manipulate the other person to do the lesson for her.

These behaviors made it difficult for classmates to interact with Nicole. For example, during a game that involved drawing boxes on paper, Nicole was assigned to work with Bud. Nicole and Bud had not been selected by other classmates to play the game because the others considered them to be less competent partners for this game. Bud's inadequate command of English, a second language for him, was his handicap, while Nicole's visual impairment was hers. An aide supervised the game between Bud and Nicole, but Nicole appeared to take no interest in the activity. She ignored Bud's moves during the game, had to be prompted to take each turn, and caused a number of delays. Both Bud and the aide were frustrated with Nicole's behavior.

Nicole sometimes used her visual impairment to try to manipulate classmates. For example, during an art activity, she indicated she wanted to make a papier-mâché monster similar to one made by a classmate, so the aide sat her next to Bud as he worked on his monster. However, Nicole did not pay attention to what Bud was doing, and the aide told her four times, "Bud is showing you." Nicole first asked Bud to make the monster for her, but when the aide stated that Bud could not do the entire project for Nicole, Nicole asked the aide to do it. Fortunately, Nicole's teacher had established high and consistent expectations for Nicole, so her classmates and aides did not give in to these demands.

The effects that positive feedback had on Nicole's ability to work on tasks that required attention to visual detail were dramatically demonstrated during an art activity. While making a picture of a cheetah, a classmate complimented Nicole's work with, "That's the best picture you drew, Nicole." After this remark, Nicole concentrated on her work for a longer time than we had ever before observed, and when she finished her picture, she said excitedly to classmates, "Look at this. Look what I've made!" It was important for Nicole to receive positive feedback in addition to corrections of her work, since many of her past endeavors met with failure and she needed to concentrate harder and make more of an effort to perform relatively simple tasks.

FACTORS AFFECTING SOCIAL INTEGRATION

Of the six children we observed, only two experienced some degree of acceptance by their peers, as measured by the sociometric data, and only one of the six engaged in interactions whose rate and complexity were comparable to those of sighted classmates. The remaining five children had significantly fewer opportunities to play with classmates and, therefore, fewer opportunities to acquire the kind of language and social skills that are important for acceptance by peers.

The mainstreaming experiences of these students placed unique demands on the students, the classroom teachers, and the resource-room teachers. Each mainstreaming experience required an individual response from the teachers, yet some common factors affected the outcome of the experiences of all the students. Figure 1 illustrates the complex relationship among these factors.

Characteristics of Blind and Visually Impaired Students
Language and Social Skills
Although the six children varied in the extent of their vision loss, we found no simple relationship between the degree of visual impairment and integration into the regular education classroom. Rather, the children's language and social skills played a greater role in their involvement with their classmates than did their visual impairment. It was important for the students to be able to initiate conversations and to talk, not only about themselves, but about their classmates' interests. It was also important that they be able to join play groups that were already in progress. Indirect strategies for entry, including listening to the children in the play group and producing similar behaviors, followed by direct strategies, increased the likelihood of acceptance into play groups.

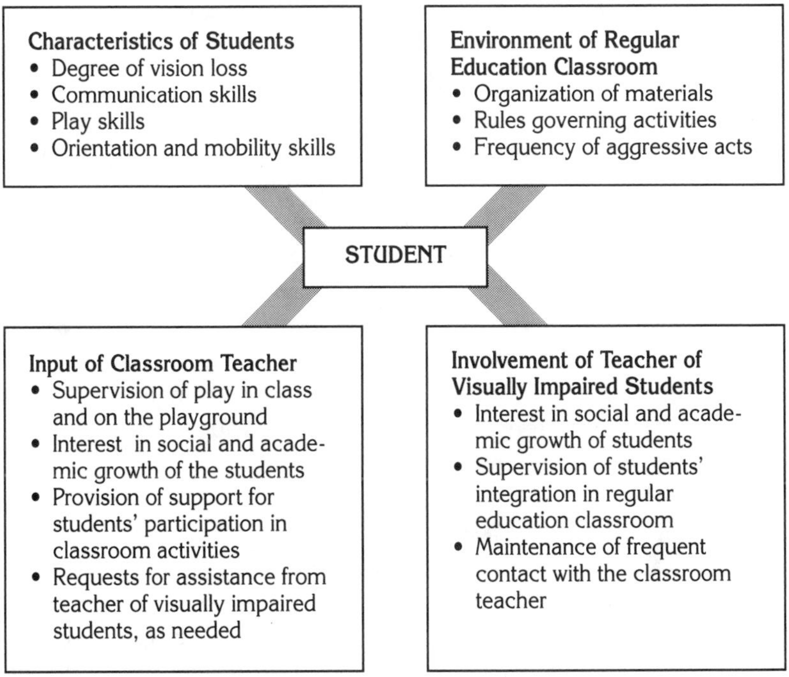

Characteristics of Students
- Degree of vision loss
- Communication skills
- Play skills
- Orientation and mobility skills

Environment of Regular Education Classroom
- Organization of materials
- Rules governing activities
- Frequency of aggressive acts

STUDENT

Input of Classroom Teacher
- Supervision of play in class and on the playground
- Interest in social and academic growth of the students
- Provision of support for students' participation in classroom activities
- Requests for assistance from teacher of visually impaired students, as needed

Involvement of Teacher of Visually Impaired Students
- Interest in social and academic growth of students
- Supervision of students' integration in regular education classroom
- Maintenance of frequent contact with the classroom teacher

Figure 1. Model of Social Integration for Visually Impaired Students.

The six children's visual impairments affected their abilities to monitor the attention of their sighted classmates. Since classmates came and left without announcing their arrivals and departures, the visually impaired children sometimes talked to classmates who were not present or who were not attending to them. Sighted students sometimes talked to their visually impaired classmates when they were engrossed in an activity. On these occasions, the visually impaired students often failed to listen or respond to class-mates' questions and invitations to play. To reduce these break-downs in interactions, teachers can remind sighted classmates to identify themselves by name or to greet a blind or visually impaired child when they arrive at a play scene and to announce their departures verbally. By role playing with blindfolds, sighted students can experience the silent arrivals and departures of class-mates. When breakdowns in communication occur, children need to be encouraged to repair them by initiating conversations with their partners' names, repeating a question or comment that is not initially answered, or trying to improve the message.

During kindergarten and first grade, many unstructured interac-tions involve play with toys. The children we observed varied con-siderably in their abilities to use objects appropriately. Some used toys for self-stimulation and some used toys appropriately by themselves, but the children who were most successfully main-streamed played with toys with classmates. Although the play skills of most sighted children develop without an inordinate amount of intervention from adults, the play skills of blind and visually impaired children are often delayed. Hence, classroom teachers may need to help visually impaired students become familiar with toys used by classmates and to help them play with these toys with their classmates. They may also wish to find out from parents which toys the visually impaired students are able to play with appropriately at home and to introduce some of these toys into classroom interactions.

Orientation and Mobility Skills

The orientation and mobility skills of the visually impaired children also affected their abilities to interact with classmates. We found that the severely impaired students' inability to keep up with class-mates made it especially hard for them to play with others on the playground and that these children needed a few minutes head start. For those who were isolated on the playground, games that were organized and supervised by teachers provided opportunities for them to interact with sighted classmates. When a teacher could not supervise such activities, an activity table with toys of interest to both types of children provided a place to come together and focus on similar interests and, consequently, increased the rate of positive interactions. By providing objects that were novel to students during two or three recess periods each week, the classroom teachers were able to maintain the children's interest in continuing the activity.

Role of the Classroom Teacher

The visually impaired children who had the most positive mainstreaming experience had teachers who regarded their students' social development to be as important as their academic achievement and who promoted positive interactions among their students. For these students, it was critical that their classroom teachers closely monitored their interactions throughout the school year. In some cases, interactions between the visually impaired student and sighted classmates had started on a generally positive note, but had decreased in frequency over time or had become troublesome. In these instances, it was important that the classroom teacher quickly identify the problem and intercede before negative patterns of interaction became firmly established. Sometimes, the private conversations we overheard revealed important information about the visually impaired child's standing among classmates. While classroom teachers have numerous academic goals to achieve, it is also crucial that they make time in their schedules to listen to the conversations of their students. The teachers who found time to do so also had intellectually stimulating classrooms. They found ways to meet the academic goals without sacrificing the social development of their students.

The kind of classroom environment created by the classroom teacher had a profound effect on the mainstreaming experience. Of the six children, those who were accepted by classmates and had opportunities to interact with them were placed in classrooms in which the size of play groups was restricted, the initiation and termination of activities were governed by rules, and activities were carefully selected by the classroom teachers. Although most of the sighted children in the five classrooms we observed were able to join in activities with classmates, it was a difficult task for the visually impaired students to do so. Some classroom teachers facilitated this process by setting up activity centers in the classroom and assigning groups of children to these centers. Thus, classroom teachers must give special consideration to the sighted classmates who are chosen to participate in activities with blind or visually impaired students. Sighted classmates must not only be skilled in the target task, they must be able to encourage the blind or visually impaired student to participate in activities.

Over the course of the field study, we found that classroom teachers differed in their abilities to recognize the special needs of the less severely visually impaired students. When initially interviewed, the teachers commented on how similar these students were to their sighted classmates, but they differed tremendously in how they worked with these children. One classroom teacher talked about the student's visual impairment with the sighted children as the need arose and made certain that a classroom aide or sighted student was available to assist the visually impaired student when tasks required attention to visual information. In another classroom, the teacher never talked with students about their visually impaired classmate's special needs and did not offer sufficient assistance when games and academic lessons required greater visual acuity than the student possessed. The visually impaired students in these two classrooms had different school experiences. The first was able to participate in many of the conversations and games of her classmates and made social gains during the school year, whereas the second experienced a number of failures in his social and academic endeavors.

Role of the Resource-Room Teacher

The resource-room teachers played a significant role in the degree to which all six children participated in both academic and social endeavors. When the input of resource-room teachers, the abilities of the visually impaired students, and the quality of the education in the regular education classroom were optimal, the mainstreaming experience of the students was positive. In most cases, however, the children had cognitive or social deficits that their classroom teachers did not know how to address. It was critical for resource-room teachers to work with teachers on these sources of trouble in the classroom, as well as on their own agendas in the resource room. Since social experiences are as important as academic skills learned in the resource room, the resource-room teacher, through periodic monitoring of interactions in the classroom and playground, could identify problems overlooked by the classroom teacher and could suggest ways to improve these situations.

It is important that the assistance provided by the resource-room teacher to the regular education teacher continue throughout the school year. In some classrooms, resource-room teachers held an in-service session for the classroom teacher and the sighted students at the beginning of the school year but did not return regularly to remedy new problems that arose or to refresh students on skills they had forgotten over time. The mainstreaming experiences that were most beneficial to the visually impaired students were characterized by a close relationship between the resource-room teacher and the classroom teacher. Conversations were frequent, and sources of trouble were quickly identified and remedied.

It is also important for teachers who have large caseloads in the resource room and who have little time to work on social skills in the classroom to promote positive interactions and relationships among the blind and visually impaired students in the resource room.

Last, resource-room teachers should be encouraged to play an active role in placing blind and visually impaired students in regular education classrooms. We found that the interest expressed by classroom teachers did not ensure positive mainstreaming experiences for the students we observed. After examining assessment records and interviewing the students, resource-room teachers should understand the students' needs. With this information, they should be encouraged by school administrators to identify classroom teachers who can best meet these special needs most effectively.

Contextual Demands

The ability of the visually impaired students to participate in classroom activities and to interact with classmates was influenced by various factors: the number of participants, the location of the event, the specific type of activity involved, the sighted classmates selected as partners, and the amount of support provided by the classroom teacher.

When students were allowed to make their own arrangements for membership in play and work activities, we observed more conflicts in the classroom. For blind and visually impaired students, it is important to limit the number of children who work and play together. Doing so will not only improve the classroom environment overall, but will make it **eas**ier for the blind or visually impaired student to get to know and interact with classmates. We observed that the most positive benefits were derived when classroom teachers paired the visually impaired student with a socially skilled classmate for academic and social tasks.

In general, we found it was more difficult for the visually impaired children to play and converse with classmates on the playground than in the classroom because of the noise and activity level. Thus, blind and visually impaired students need greater assistance if they are to benefit from free play outside. In the classroom, quiet space is necessary so they can play with a few classmates. A loft area or a corner in the classroom can be closed off, so there is less traffic and less chance of disruption.

When activities require access to visual information, it is critical that classroom teachers adapt materials and supervise these activities so the blind or visually impaired students can participate. We observed considerable variability in sighted children's skills at playing and working with their blind classmates. Thus, it is important that appropriate children are selected as partners so all the students have a positive learning experience.

Finally, it is crucial that teachers closely monitor their students' conversations and interactions. The demands that the visually impaired students faced and the assistance required to help each child truly become a part of the educational mainstream were unique. The quality of their mainstreaming experience was determined, to a large extent, by their teachers' willingness to listen to their private conversations, to observe their interactions with classmates, and to help them with their special needs.

CONCLUSION

The challenge of interacting with peers is considerable for blind and visually impaired children, and many face rejection when mainstreamed. If teachers are to identify those who are at risk of unsuccessful mainstreaming and are to implement effective interventions, it is imperative that in-depth studies of the children's interactions with their peers be conducted. In the study described here, we identified some of the unique concerns of the visually impaired students we observed. On the basis of our observations, we developed guidelines for mainstreaming blind and visually impaired students, which are presented in Chapter 7, so teachers can be more successful in promoting the social development of these children and improving their social standing among classmates.

Chapter 5

The Social Acceptance and Interaction of Visually Impaired Children in Integrated Settings

P. Ann MacCuspie

Integration is not a culture-free concept; it is laden with basic assumptions and values. Therefore, implementation of and resistance to integration should be viewed in relation to the cultural change it entails. When visually impaired students are enrolled in regular classrooms, contradictions and dilemmas are created as people struggle to accommodate to or resist the inevitable changes that are inherent in integration. The social environment of the elementary school is complex. Therefore, if integration of visually impaired students is to be realized, leadership is critical for the creation and modification of a culture that will enhance the acceptance of the changes entailed, as well as for the acknowledgment and confrontation of the philosophical and pragmatic issues that are intrinsic to integration. As Scott (1969b, p. 14) contended:

> The disability of blindness is a learned social role. The various attitudes and patterns of behavior that characterize people who are blind are not inherent in their condition but, rather, are acquired through ordinary processes of social learning ...the same processes of socialization that have made us all.

Through an exploration of the social interaction and perceptions of students and adults involved with the students, the studies reported here, which were conducted at five different sites, bring into view aspects of the pupil culture and the school culture that shape the social integration of visually impaired children. An analysis of contradictions and dilemmas makes visible the ways in which the school environment can be hostile to the integrated visually impaired student.

THEORETICAL FRAMEWORK

Much of the research on the social adaptation of people with visual impairments has focused on the deficits identified as characteristic of this group, such as inappropriate behaviors and limited access to nonverbal cues. The structuring aspects of the social environment, the complexities of social interaction, the interactive nature of interpersonal relationships, and the impact of society's treatment of people with visual impairments as an inferior minority are only implicit in some of this research. Thus, the emphasis has not been on the process of social interaction or its context.

Inherent in the concept of normalization is the belief that disabled people will have an opportunity to participate in the everyday world of the culture in which they reside. For school-aged children with disabilities, integration into the normal surroundings of public school classrooms necessitates integration into the social world of their nondisabled peers. Researchers (Davies, 1982; Glassner, 1976; Hammersley & Woods, 1984) who have focused on the culture of school-aged children contend that "children (and adolescents) maintain a social system relatively autonomous from adults" (Fine, 1981, p. 29). This social world, known as *pupil culture*, is the one the integrated visually impaired child encounters.

The study presented in this chapter was an initial exploration of the social environment encountered by integrated visually impaired students and of some of the perspectives of participants who are intimately involved in the process. The aim was to gain insight into how visually impaired students, through interactions with their sighted peers, are received in the pupil culture.

Two theoretical frameworks guided this research—symbolic interactionism and organizational culture. With regard to the concept of organizational culture, the researcher attempts to reveal those cultural assumptions that underpin people's perceptions and actions (Schein, 1985). According to the symbolic interactionist perspective, "people act on the basis of meaning and understanding which they develop through interaction with others" (Pollard,

1985, p. x). Pupil culture is the social context within which the integrated visually impaired child will be socialized. Visual impairment affects the messages and hence the meanings the student may receive. In turn, others in the student's environment interpret these meanings and construct courses of action based on their interpretations. Together, the concepts of organizational culture and symbolic interactionism provide a broad but powerful perspective from which to explore the social integration of visually impaired students.

METHODOLOGY

This multisite case-study of five different classrooms located throughout the provinces of Nova Scotia and New Brunswick in Canada involved five children, four who were partially sighted and one who was totally blind; they were randomly selected from an identified population of approximately 44 pupils. These elementary school children had a visual acuity of 20/200 or less in the better eye after correction, were without additional disabilities, were achieving at grade level or within one year of grade level, and did not demonstrate behavioral problems. Two students were enrolled at the same school but in different grades and classrooms.

The five sites observed for this research proved to have many things in common as well as both subtle and obvious differences. The schools were located in rural and in urban areas. Different grade levels, administrative arrangements, teaching strategies, and approaches to learning and discipline were noted. In examining the context associated with the perspectives of those within a given situation, many events were recorded and observed—at one site the principal resigned, at another there were troubled relations with the local school board, in one class a friend of the visually impaired student moved away. Such diversity from site to site emphasizes the importance of situational context in the lives of participants and the dynamic nature of this context.

Common to each of the five sites was the enrollment of a visually impaired pupil in a regular classroom with sighted peers. An itinerant teacher for visually impaired students provided instructional assistance to the visually impaired pupil and programming consultation to the classroom teachers several times a week. In all sites, the classroom teachers were responsible for the visually impaired student for more than 80 percent of the school day, excluding the noon-hour recess.

As is characteristic of qualitative research, participant observation, interviews, and documents were used in the collection and analysis of data. Approximately five months, one in each classroom with an integrated student, were spent at the sites in collecting data through participant observations and formal and informal interviews with the visually impaired students, five to eight of their classmates, their teachers, their itinerant teachers, the school principals, and parents. Documents available at the site (newsletters, individualized educational programs, report cards, and procedural manuals, for example) and those relevant to integration published by provincial departments of education were analyzed.

While transcribing interviews and reviewing participant-observation notes, categories and themes relative to the research concerns were identified, and then codes were created for emerging themes, insights, and information related to specific research questions, key concepts, and common patterns, both within and across. After all the data were coded, they were compared. As patterns and interrelationships emerged, the links among the concepts were specified and refined. Triangulation was used to confirm findings; thus, accounts and observations were validated by using three or more different methods (observation, interviews, informal discussions, and documents) to examine an issue or theme.

The cultural inferences constructed during data collection and the initial interpretation and analysis were repeatedly tested to ascertain whether they represented the students' perspectives and whether the cultural assumptions had been accurately translated. Basic assumptions of pupil culture related to friendship, acceptance, and peer interaction were identified, and the perceptions of both the visually impaired students and their classmates were examined in relation to these basic assumptions. Similarly, assumptions of adult culture that were relevant to the social acceptance and interaction of the integrated visually impaired students were identified, and the perceptions of teachers, principals, and parents were considered in relation to them. Educational assumptions with regard to the social environment encountered by integrated visually impaired students were identified and examined. Finally, contextual aspects or processes, both beyond the elementary school setting (the stigma of visual impairment, provincial legislation, or guidelines relevant to integration) and within the elementary school setting (the learning environment, emphasis on affective education) that appeared to contribute to or detract from the social acceptance and interaction of integrated visually impaired students were analyzed.

OBSERVATIONS AND PERCEPTIONS OF THE VISUALLY IMPAIRED CHILDREN

Interactions with Sighted Classmates

The visually impaired children's interactions varied in both quantity and quality from those of many of their sighted classmates. The consequences of limited vision were evident as these children struggled to locate friends on the playground, compete at similar levels, and complete schoolwork in time to participate in the "between activity" social interactions. The visually impaired children emphasized two significant criteria for friends—"they don't make fun of my eyesight" and "if I have problems they'll help me out." For sighted children, the most important criteria for friends were that they "hang around with you" and "are fun." In interaction with their peers, the visually impaired students had limited access to information about both their own levels of competence and that of their peers. This limitation seemed to contribute to the visually impaired children's belief that sighted people are superior and made it difficult for them to derive an accurate comparison of their performance and that of their sighted peers.

The visually impaired children were reluctant to join activities they perceived as too difficult, too dangerous, or requiring a high level of skill. For the boys in particular, this reluctance contributed to their perception that other boys were inaccessible to them, and they often played with girls as an alternative to being alone. All the visually impaired children routinely interacted with classmates who were outside the most popular group; it seemed that their main objective was to have someone with whom to play.

The students' visual impairments were a source of shame to them. Their confusion about the concept of disability appeared to have been constructed from the subtle, negative messages they received from peers, teachers, and parents and from their limited knowledge of their visual impairments. They attributed their exclusion from particular activities by their peers to their visual impairments and so perceived their visual impairments as posing a problems for their friends, as well as for their parents and teachers.

The children thought that their likes and dislikes were generally similar to those of their peers, but that their vision loss created academic hardships for them and hindered the process of making friends. Even those with obvious mannerisms did not perceive their behaviors to be different from those of their peers. Therefore, they did not appear to be receiving accurate feedback of their peers' negative, nonverbal responses to their inappropriate behaviors. Another obstacle to accurate feedback was the classmates' reluctance to display overt negative responses to the visually impaired children's inappropriate actions because adults frequently reprimanded them for making derogatory remarks about other children.

Perceptions of Friendship

The willingness of classmates to help them was an important consideration for the integrated students. Although they considered those who helped to be their friends, they thought their options in choosing playmates were limited. Furthermore, they all expressed a yearning to play with classmates they perceived as popular, but none routinely interacted with these popular classmates.

An important aspect of pupil culture is the requirement that children follow rules, both explicit and implicit. Although four of the visually impaired children said they followed the rules of both pupil culture and their teachers, they sensed that they had a degree of impunity because they were visually impaired. They perceived themselves to be "special" and in some situations entitled to privileges (such as going first on line) that were not available to their peers.

Another assumption of pupil culture is that friends ought to reciprocate the actions of their peers, whether negative or positive. In this regard, the visually impaired children's perceptions differed from those of their peers in three ways. First, in relation to negative encounters with peers, they thought that because of their visual impairments, their peers' treatment of them was not as harsh as it was for other children. Second, the children perceived assistance that was received as a consequence of being visually impaired (such as going to the office to enlarge a handout or helping them locate something) to be different from help obtained to complete a task unrelated to the consequences of being visually impaired (such as solving a math problem). In the former situation, the children appeared to consider the assistance as indistinguishable from the particular activity and did not acknowledge, reciprocate, or even thank the peer who had volunteered it. In the latter case, the children perceived the peers' contributions as "helping" and routinely thanked or acknowledged those who helped. Finally, the students perceived themselves as having few opportunities to reciprocate assistance from peers.

OBSERVATIONS AND PERCEPTIONS OF SIGHTED CLASSMATES

Knowledge of Visual Impairment

Each group of peers encountered one visually impaired student in the classroom. In each case, the child's classmates had limited knowledge of the child's actual visual abilities and disabilities. In the classroom, the child's visual impairment was perceived to be something "we don't talk about." Thus, conjecture was prevalent as the classmates interpreted their associations and interactions with their visually impaired classmate. In addition, their perceptions of their visually impaired classmate were marked by inconsistencies and contradictions. During interviews, they frequently described their visually impaired classmate as "just like normal persons," yet they expressed a sense of marked difference between themselves and the visually impaired child. Visually impaired children were perceived to need more attention, receive more help, be less competent, have some immunity from "being picked on," and generally seemed to wish they could see as "well as the other kids."

The label "visually impaired" seemed to have a significant and negative effect on the classmates, particularly on their perceptions of a visually impaired child's level of competence and the number of activities in which he or she could participate. One of the most significant drawbacks the classmates associated with interaction with a visually impaired classmate was the extra effort such interaction was perceived to entail. To function as a "best friend" for a visually impaired child seemed to necessitate a degree of self-sacrifice.

The classmates interpreted the slower working rate and the large, often "messy-looking" appearance of the visually impaired child's handiwork as evidence of incompetence or of a lower level of ability. In addition, although they considered adaptive materials necessary or helpful for the visually impaired child they thought that work completed using adaptive materials or equipment was of a lesser quality or less mature than that produced through regular means. By the upper elementary levels, the sighted children were beginning to perceive their visually impaired classmate's use of equipment (such as a closed-circuit television, computer, or tape recorder) as providing an unfair advantage. This perception was particularly evident in competitive learning environments.

The sighted children thought that the visually impaired classmate had different friends than did most students—less popular children in the class or children from other classes. In a qualitative study of disabled students' level of social acceptance, Jones and Chiba (1985) reported that nondisabled peers rated the visually impaired students (fourth- to sixth-graders) as being less popular and socially savvy than other groups of disabled students in the study. Also, the nondisabled students thought that the visually impaired boys chose to play with girls more frequently than did their male classmates. In addition, the visually impaired students seemed to be in a neutral position with regard to popularity: neither sought out by classmates, as were popular children, nor the brunt of teasing and tormenting, as were many unpopular children.

Few sighted classmates spontaneously reported that the visually impaired child acted differently from other children in their class. However, they did say that the visually impaired children "looked different." When asked specifically about these children's "different behavior," their responses centered on the mannerisms typically associated with visually impaired children, including arm flapping or jumping about when excited, not making eye contact, or standing too close when speaking with someone. Furthermore, they thought these different behaviors were undesirable. For example, the lack of eye contact from the visually impaired child during interaction was considered to be blatant disrespect.

Sighted Peers as Helpers

Each group of sighted students believed that its visually impaired classmate required a substantial amount of help. Although they were not "best friends" with the visually impaired student, classmates felt they were obligated or at least expected routinely provide to assistance. Even when a visually impaired child was paired with a less capable student for a particular activity and completed the major part of the assignment, the sighted classmate perceived this situation as one in which he or she had been helping the visually impaired student.

Within pupil culture, friends are expected to reciprocate the actions of their friends, whether positive or negative. Visually impaired children presented predicaments for sighted classmates in this regard. The sighted classmates felt uncomfortable or unable to reciprocate negative actions, such as hitting or "telling on" the visually impaired child. They also saw major difficulties in the visually impaired child's reciprocating the help the sighted students routinely provided. In addition, they thought that their visually impaired classmate was receiving special treatment and privileges from the teachers. They even suspected that the visually impaired child was "faking" his or her visual impairment to get this "special treatment."

OBSERVATIONS AND PERCEPTIONS OF ADULTS

Integration challenged the adults' basic assumptions of the social acceptance and interaction of children, as well as the interaction of teachers and children. Frequently, the adults struggled with the complexities of accommodating visually impaired children's disabilities in a fair manner yet not treating the children "differently." They did not fully understand the implications of vision loss on social and academic learning, and they were conditioned to view acknowledgment of a child's disability as inappropriate.

Integration posed particular dilemmas for teachers, who considered children's social acceptance by peers to be an aspect of child development that occurs naturally during interactions, not a major responsibility of teachers. The predominant role of the teacher, they believed, is to prevent children from mistreating each other, not to promote positive interactions or enhance the development of a healthy self-concept. In general, children were considered responsible for making their own friends, and playgrounds were almost neutral environments for teachers.

The parents thought that their visually impaired children were responsible for making friends, yet they were unaware of the "different interactions" of their children during free play on the playground. Rather, they assumed their children were adequately accepted and actively involved with friends at these times. Both the teachers and parents generally based their perceptions of the visually impaired children's social acceptance on the absence of classmates' physical or verbal abuse of the children, not on the presence or absence of positive social experiences.

Adults were oblivious to many of the assumptions of pupil culture that affected the acceptance or rejection of children by their peers. Despite the best intentions, this ignorance frequently resulted in actions that hindered the children's acceptance, such as asking a classmate to play with a visually impaired student during recess. The teachers also seemed oblivious to the ways in which they treated visually impaired children differently from their peers. Their expectations for the children's level of performance were sometimes inappropriate; they introduced activities that were meaningless without access to more accurate visual information; and, on several occasions, they expected the children to participate in activities that posed a significant risk to their safety.

Most of the adults mentioned the stigma that is perceived to be associated with those who are visually impaired. They felt sorry for visually impaired people and believed that visually impaired people are more courageous than are fully sighted people. Furthermore, they were convinced that the particular visually impaired student with whom they were acquainted was "exceptional" and hence encountered less difficulty coping with the regular curriculum than would most other visually impaired students.

Both the teachers and the parents thought that the visually impaired children's appearance hampered the children's acceptance by peers. (The parents seemed tormented by the different appearance of their children, as if it were an inescapable symbol of their children's disability.) However, the parents and teachers had different perceptions of the mannerisms of the visually impaired students. The teachers tended to ignore even blatantly inappropriate mannerisms and seemed to think that addressing the mannerisms would call attention to or emphasize the child's disability. Since many claimed that they had not heard other students comment on these mannerisms, they thought the sighted students either were not interested in them or had simply accepted them. The parents, on the other hand, considered their children's mannerisms to be a major problem that had to be dealt with regularly.

The discussion of visual impairment, especially in the presence of a visually impaired child and other students, was another problem for the adults. Perhaps because it was impossible to ignore the accommodations required for a totally blind child, as one could those of a partially sighted child, those who were involved with a totally blind child were less inhibited when issues related to visual impairment were mentioned spontaneously. In general, adults struggled when the topic of visual impairment was raised and were visibly uncomfortable discussing it, even during the interviews.

THE BROADER SOCIAL CONTEXT

Three processes evident in the broader context in which elementary schools are located appeared to be relevant to the social acceptance and interaction of the integrated visually impaired children in the study: (1) integration as an educational innovation implemented through the schools, (2) affective education as an aim of education, and (3) society's perception of the stigma associated with visual impairment. Assumptions of social acceptance and interaction of integrated blind and visually impaired children that are related to these broader processes served to make some beginning connections between macrosociological processes and the individual students' experiences.

Integration as Innovation

Both the inadequate training of teachers before the integration of a visually impaired student and the lack of formal evaluation of integration as it was being implemented suggested that the education system is not strongly committed to integration. This lack of commitment, together with the routine lack of even basic textbooks in accessible formats, such as braille or large print, contributes to the perception that integrated visually impaired students are less valued than are sighted students.

Other evidence of the lack of commitment to integration were the limited input of teachers in the planning and implementation of integration and the absence of a coordinated or team approach to integration. Without such an approach at all five sites, it would be difficult for teachers to have a significant effect upon the social acceptance and interaction of integrated visually impaired students. For instance, itinerant teachers who were in the schools only at specific times had little opportunity to observe the social skills of the children during free-play periods and thus were not aware of this aspect of the children's school life. Furthermore, the teachers had not developed uniform strategies for dealing with mannerisms that interfered with interaction. When a child mastered a skill in the classroom, other teachers were not informed and so continued to provide support the child no longer needed. Moreover, the teachers did not change their programs or, in the majority of cases, significantly adjust their presentation of material or information to accommodate the visually impaired students.

Affective Education as an Educational Aim

The lack of commitment to affective education in the elementary schools created difficulties when issues inherent to the social integration of visually impaired students were examined. Teachers had neither the training nor the insight to address issues involved in the social acceptance and interaction relevant to the visually impaired students. Furthermore, their social and academic expectations of the visually impaired students were lower than their expectations of the sighted children, and they thus assumed that these children would not be well accepted by their sighted peers.

The administrators and teachers did not seem to be concerned about the children's friendships in general. When they assigned children to classes, their intent was to create a mixed group of children of different levels of ability or to separate students who were a "bad influence" on each other. Therefore, class assignments appeared to address the teachers' need for control, not to enhance the positive relationships or existing friendships of children.

Stigma of Visual Impairment

The presence of a visual impairment functioned as a "label of primary potency" (Allport, 1958) that influenced the perceptions of all who were involved with the integrated visually impaired children. This stigma is inherent in the way society perceives those who are visually impaired and the potential they have as students in public schools. It obscures the perceptions of others and contributes to lower expectations for the social, physical, and academic performance of visually impaired students.

THE CONTEXT OF ELEMENTARY SCHOOLS

There were conceivably hundreds of aspects of the situation that appeared to influence, either positively or negatively, the sighted individuals' perceptions in relation to the social acceptance and interaction of these children. Each school appeared to have contextual facets that contributed to unique circumstances in the school (such as the threats to safety of a visually impaired child because of congestion in the playground). However, some processes were common to all the schools (for instance, the expectation that children who were different from their peers would be less acceptable to their classmates). In addition, an aspect that was especially potent at one school was sometimes unremarkable in a different context. Thus, the degree and intensity of a single variable seemed to fluctuate as an inextricably interwoven aspect of a given context.

Contextual issues were grouped into six categories, factors that were relevant primarily to: (1) the individual visually impaired student (level of maturity, social skills, and type of vision loss), (2) sighted classmates (physical prowess and academic ability), (3) teachers (teaching style and degree to which they were supportive of the concept of integration), (4) classroom environments (type of learning environment and seating arrangements), (5) administrative arrangements (use of a team approach and perceived level of principals' commitment to integration), and (6) the structure of playgrounds (availability of activities suitable for visually impaired children and the size and congestion of space). In given contexts, these social factors could together constrain or enable the social acceptance and interaction of integrated blind and visually impaired students.

CONTRADICTIONS AND DILEMMAS

The basic assumptions of a culture are established when a visually impaired student is enrolled in an elementary school. Understood principles, standards, and beliefs guide how students learn, work, and play, as well as how teachers control and teach their students. In the research reported here, the integration of the visually impaired students challenged the intrinsic philosophies and practices of school life. Children and adults were expected to assume new roles and responsibilities. Procedures that were once routine became problematic when one member of the class could not see the chalkboard, decipher the diagrams, or find favorite classmates in the playground.

As contradictions and dilemmas were identified, so were the potential implications for the integrated students. Two significant contradictions, evident in all five schools, appeared to detract from the social acceptance and interaction of these students. Both were related to the incompatibility between the philosophical implications of integration and the cultural assumptions held by those in schools. The first contradiction was that despite the goal of integration, being different was viewed negatively and acceptance of difference was neither routinely promoted nor enhanced. The second contradiction was between the concept of individualized programming and progress inherent in integration and the competitive learning environments of and group instruction provided in the classrooms.

The dilemmas associated with the social acceptance and interaction of integrated students were related to the use of adaptive equipment, materials, and teaching strategies; the types of adaptive behaviors developed by the visually impaired students; the uneasiness of adults in discussing visual impairment; the relationship between program adaptations and the inclusion of the visually impaired students; the accessibility of friends to the visually impaired students; and the pressures on and responsibilities of teachers. Actions that were considered appropriate or critical to accommodate the unique learning needs of visually impaired students (such as using a white cane) were sometimes disruptive of the student's social integration (for example, classmates were asked not to speak to visually impaired students when they were traveling independently with their canes). Therefore, the visually impaired students had to choose between such things as competent performance and social interaction. The adults' discomfort with open, spontaneous discussion of a visually impaired student's disability frequently resulted in the students' ignoring necessary program adaptations—accommodations for the student. Teachers were reluctant to be seen to be "drawing attention" to a child's disability, yet the student's competent performance was jeopardized without the necessary adaptations.

The major implication of these contradictions and dilemmas was the risk to the integrated students' developing self-concept. Being visually impaired was a predominant aspect of these children's being. During their school life, scarcely a minute passed when some compensatory skill or accommodating action was not required if they were to participate with their peers. The children thought that their control over their actions was significantly restricted by their visual impairment, and the danger was that their less-than-desirable level of acceptance by and interaction with peers would be perceived as an inevitable consequence of being visually impaired.

Despite their different levels of maturity, visual impairment, age, and social skills, the children had acquired some common beliefs about blindness and visual impairment and about people who are blind or visually impaired. These beliefs include the following:

- Blind and visually impaired people must depend on sighted people for help.
- Visually impaired people need more help to do most things than sighted people do.
- Sighted people can do more things than can visually impaired people.
- Sighted people can do most things better than can visually impaired people.
- Sighted people are thankful they are not visually impaired.
- Visually impaired people are different and hence inferior to sighted people.
- Sighted people think they are superior to visually impaired people.
- Sighted people think visually impaired people are not as intelligent as they are.
- Being visually impaired causes extra problems for parents and teachers.
- Parents wish their children were not visually impaired.
- Sighted children prefer to play with other sighted children.
- Visually impaired children are less desirable as "best friends" than are those who are fully sighted.

As the self-concepts of these children were gradually evolving during the process of social interaction, the beliefs just listed were prominent. Thus, one of the more significant implications for integrated visually impaired students was the potential threat to their development of a positive self-concept.

DISCUSSION

This exploratory research began with some fundamental premises about the concept of integration, its relation to society as a whole, the socialization role of schools, the ways in which school participants construct their social reality, the structuring aspects of the social environment of schools and those of processes external to the school, the development of self-concept, the potential restrictions that visual impairment imposes upon interaction, and the response of individuals to change. All these premises are relevant to the culture evolving in the social environments of schools. Culture is pervasive, complex, and difficult to analyze. Changes, such as integration, must address the cultural implications they entail.

Although the students chosen for this multiple-site study were selected from a relatively small geographic area in Canada and represented a homogeneous ethnic group, the observational data strongly suggest outcomes similar to those in Kekelis and Sacks's (1988) study with respect to the integration of blind and visually impaired students and the perceptions of parents and teachers. Even though the age range of students in the present research was more diverse, common themes regarding the visually impaired students' social acceptance by peers and their interactions with regular education teachers seem to emerge.

The conclusions drawn from this research parallel those of Kekelis and Sacks (1988). Overall, it appears that integration of students with visual impairments has been implemented without consideration of the complex philosophical and pragmatic issues that are inherent in this process. The basic assumptions of school culture, particularly those relevant to social integration, are challenged by and are frequently incompatible with the process of integration. Therefore, tensions, contradictions, and dilemmas evolve for all participants. For the visually impaired students, in particular, a potentially hostile social environment is evident. Both the teachers and classmates seem to tolerate the integrated students, rather than truly accept their differences.

The adults had only a limited understanding of the complexity and nature of pupil culture—the primary context within which all students must function—and its relevance to the social integration of visually impaired students. Therefore, they sometimes unintentionally place visually impaired students in situations that hinder their acceptance in this culture.

The interactions of visually impaired students vary in both quality and quantity from those of many of their sighted classmates, and the pervasive negative influence of the label "visually impaired," as well as the direct effects of visual impairment on communication, are evident. The sighted students perceived visually impaired students to be less competent, less desirable as friends or workmates, more dependent, in need of more assistance, and less popular than other students, and the visually impaired students' perceptions of themselves were similar. Hence, the developing self-concept of integrated visually impaired children must be considered at risk in the social environments of many elementary schools.

Many aspects of the elementary school context have impact on the social acceptance and interaction of integrated visually impaired students. Particular contextual aspects (such as seating arrangements) contribute to unique circumstances within any school. Broader processes, including the low priority given to affective education in elementary schools; inadequate and inaccurate information about a student's visual impairment and its implications; and a vast number of factors inherent in the school culture, such as reduced expectations for the performance of disabled students, influence the social interaction and acceptance of visually impaired students. Therefore, the acceptance of visually impaired students must be seen to be a multidimensional, dynamic construct that is intrinsic to the social context, not a single event fixed across time and situation.

In general, regular classrooms in which little effort is made to acknowledge the students' visual impairment and to accommodate the implications of visual impairment on the students' affective, physical, and cognitive development should be considered potentially hostile social environments. Unless the integration process takes into account the positive acceptance of difference, the specific needs of these students, and the school culture, the chance for these students to construct a positive self-image, encounter an accepting social environment, participate actively in classroom and playground activities, and enjoy their school days is at risk.

RECOMMENDATIONS

It is evident that, in the future, stronger demands will be made upon educators to accommodate a more diverse student population in the regular classroom. The following recommendations, although directed specifically toward the integration of visually impaired students, may enhance the development of the regular classroom to benefit all children.

- Considerable attention must be focused on the process of integration and on the complex philosophical, moral, and pragmatic issues inherent in this concept. Educators and parents must identify the potential effects of integration on the basic cultural assumptions of elementary school classrooms and the incompatible aspects of integrating visually impaired students. Educational leaders must help all those involved in the process to address the dilemmas that emerge, especially with regard to the emotional and social development of students and the creation of a social environment that promotes the positive acceptance of differences and eradicates the stigma of being different.

- Educators and parents need to become cognizant of the social world of children, their perspectives, and the role friendship plays in their affective development. If adults are to enhance social acceptance and interaction, they must understand the rules that children use to gain acceptance, to interact positively, and to make friends. It is only through planned intervention that visually impaired students can experience such things as reciprocating the assistance they routinely receive from sighted classmates. Such aspects of a visually impaired child's development must be considered to be as critical as are those associated with academic progress.

- Visual impairment must become a topic of both formal and informal discussions in the classrooms in which visually impaired students are integrated. Therefore, all those involved must be knowledgeable about the nature and implications of this disability. This learning should be ongoing, so the integrated students' practical and conceptual understanding expands as they mature.

- Teaching strategies and environments, such as cooperative learning, that enhance social acceptance and interaction need to be identified (Johnson & Johnson, 1981), as do those that hinder them.

- Teaching strategies must accommodate visually impaired students' limited access to or inability to use visual material by providing information in formats that the students can use. On the playground, games and activities must be planned and offered in which these children can participate and experience success. To ensure that integrated visually impaired students have the opportunity to develop a positive self-concept, schools must establish a context that emphasizes the abilities and minimizes the limitations imposed by visual impairment.

- Classroom teachers and teachers of visually impaired students must help integrated students develop social skills that are relevant to both the pupil culture and the adult world. The children must learn the rules for effective interaction and receive feedback about their sighted peers' responses to their behavior. Teachers must help these students control their mannerisms and learn how their sighted classmates react to these mannerisms.

- It is critical for educators and parents to monitor the social interaction of integrated visually impaired students. Attention should be paid to the frequency, type, and quality of these children's interactions, as well as those that are typical of sighted classmates of the same gender. Observations by parents, classroom teachers, and itinerant teachers for the visually impaired should be recorded and compared to evaluate and direct the affective development of the visually impaired students. Early and routine intervention is required to ensure that the changing needs of the students are addressed.

- The integration of visually impaired students should be perceived as a significant educational innovation requiring a formal plan of implementation. This plan must include training and in-service opportunities for classroom teachers, preparation of students, procedural guidelines, adequate funding for essential resources, and monitoring and evaluation systems. It is essential that the cultural changes that integration entails are addressed.

- Since regular classroom teachers have been designated as having the major educational responsibility for integrated visually impaired students, they should participate fully in designing programs and implementation plans. They should also be part of the ongoing decision making involved in the placement of and programming for the integrated students in their classrooms. Their involvement is necessary if integration is to become a viable educational practice.

CONCLUSION

There is much that society in general, and educators in particular, have to learn and understand about the social, instructional, and temporal integration of disabled children. Research on integration has supported the conclusion that integration is a complex innovation that requires the major restructuring of the educational system if the inherent benefits of this process are to be realized (Gall, 1987; Hatlen & Curry, 1987; Quintal, 1986). Until both the implicit and explicit issues relevant to the integration of visually impaired students are acknowledged and addressed, these students will continue to encounter a less than positive social environment in school.

However, these considerations do not imply a return to segregated educational placements for visually impaired students. To return to such placements would be to abandon the mission to change those aspects of the public school system that are incompatible with the integration of disabled students and that are barriers to the successful performance of many other students, such as unpopular and rejected children, who are considered to be "at risk" in schools. It is the professional responsibility of all educators to promote the social, physical, and cognitive development of all children.

The right to be educated in a regular classroom is one that most citizens take for granted. This right is being recognized and, in some Canadian provinces, is mandated by law for visually impaired children. What cannot be mandated is the provision of a positive learning environment—one that challenges the academic, social, and physical potential of each student; ensures the opportunity to develop a positive self-concept and high self-esteem; and that gives students the chance to experience the joys and benefits of peer friendships. If society is to realize the benefits of an integrated school system, it must improve the learning environment for all students.

Chapter 6

Peer-Mediated and Teacher-Directed Social-Skills Training for Blind and Visually Impaired Students

Sharon Zell Sacks and Robert J. Gaylord-Ross

The preceding chapters have identified a number of difficulties facing blind and visually impaired children when they are integrated into settings with sighted classmates. Recently, researchers have tried to train blind and visually impaired children using a peer-mediated approach.

Given the potential impact of social-skills training on blind and visually impaired students, we examined a critical component of this training. In past experiments, both peers and teachers were used to enhance social interaction. In the typical peer-mediated training, a teacher taught a nondisabled peer a number of ways to facilitate social interactions with a disabled peer. (The initial training, though, took place between the teacher and the peer.) The peer was then expected to use these skills with the disabled student in a free-play setting. In contrast, in teacher-directed social-skills training, an adult instructor teaches a disabled student various social behaviors. After the student has learned one or more behaviors from the teacher, he or she is expected to use them in a free-play or probe setting.

The question then arises: Which is superior—a teacher-directed procedure or a peer-mediated procedure? On the one hand, because teachers are trained in educational methods and usually have years of experience in instructing disabled students, the teacher-directed procedure may be superior for teaching social skills. On the other hand, a peer-mediated procedure in a free-play setting may lead to greater generalization of the skills that are learned. This study attempted to test these predictions.

METHOD

Participants
Visually Impaired Students
Fifteen students, aged 7–12, from four schools in three school districts in a large metropolitan area were selected to participate. All the students were congenitally visually impaired and considered legally blind, as documented by medical reports. They were of average intelligence, as measured by a standard IQ (intelligence quotient) test, and their primary impairment was visual. Students who had received prior social-skills training were excluded from the study.

All the students were educated in a resource-room program by a credentialed teacher of visually impaired students and were mainstreamed into a regular classroom environment for at least 30 percent of the school day. Students with social needs were referred by their special education teachers. Table 1 (in the appendix at the end of this chapter) presents the characteristics of the visually impaired students and the treatment groups to which they were assigned. No statistical differences (using a two-sample version of the Wilcoxon test) were apparent between the groups for level of academic performance.

Sighted Peers
Five same-age same-sex classmates of the visually impaired students were assigned to the peer-mediated approach. The students were recommended by their classroom teachers or volunteered after an in-class presentation describing the purpose of the investigation. Each sighted student was selected from the mainstream class that the visually impaired student attended. If more than one student per class was nominated or volunteered, the teacher would pick the most qualified pupil. The sighted students chosen were performing on or above grade level on academic tasks and demonstrated positive attitudes toward disabled and nondisabled classmates, as indicated by the teacher's reports.

Setting
Training Sites
The two training programs were conducted in either the resource rooms or the playgrounds of the public schools. A section of each resource room was partitioned during training sessions. All the resource rooms had similar physical arrangements. They had access to a computer system for visually impaired persons, educational games and materials, instructional aids (braillers, magnification systems, and braille and large-print texts), and free-time areas.

Probe Sites
Observational data were collected in a number of natural settings in the schools: the playgrounds during recess, the cafeterias during lunch, and the resource rooms during free-time activities.

Measurements
Behavioral Measures
Five graduate students in special education were trained to code a number of behaviors in the training or probe settings. Ten-minute observations were randomly selected from one of the probe settings each day. Baseline sessions were held on five consecutive days, and postbaseline probes were conducted three times per week. The first ten minutes of each training session were recorded. A recorder was designated to record only the probe or training session of a particular student. The recorder was aware of the treatment status of the student, but not of the specific behaviors for which the student was being trained.

The recorder stood approximately 10 feet from the visually impaired student throughout the 10-minute session. The behavioral categories were scored either according to the frequency of events (and duration) or in a Likert-scale summary score for the whole session. It was thought that rating scales would provide accurate measures while permitting the simultaneous-event recording of other measures in a reliable fashion.

On the basis of the assessment data provided by Van Hasselt, Hersen, Kazdin, Simon, and Mastanuono (1982) and initial feedback from the resource-room teachers regarding the overall social competence of the visually impaired students, the following behaviors were targeted for training:

- *Appropriate gaze* was scored when the student's head was up and positioned on a horizontal plane and turned in the direction of the peer's face during an interaction. The direction of gaze was event-recorded by frequency (number of occurrences per session) and duration. Duration was cumulatively recorded with a stopwatch. The mean duration score (per session) was calculated by dividing the total duration score for the session by the number of gaze events.

- *Body posture* was defined as the student's ability to stand or sit in an erect and natural position with his or her head forward and up. It was measured qualitatively on a seven-point Likert scale (1 = poor, 4 = fair, 7 = good) at the end of the session.

- *Positive social initiations* including some greeting or another approach response, were defined as the student's ability to start age-appropriate verbal or nonverbal interactions with sighted age-mates across school settings. Positive social initiations were event recorded according to their frequency of occurrence.

- *Joining in group activities* was defined as the student's moving into the proximity of an existing group's activity (approaching), asking to participate, and waiting for the group's approval. Each student's behavior was measured in terms of frequency (event recordings throughout the session) and qualitatively (at the end of the session) on a seven-point Likert scale (1 = poor skills, 4 = fair skills, and 7 = good skills).

- *Sharing in group activities* was defined as the student's ability to engage in an activity determined by the group: to follow the group's rules, take turns, exhibit appropriate play behavior, and adhere to the group's decisions. It was measured qualitatively on a seven-point Likert scale (1 = poor skills, 4 = fair skills, 7 = good skills) at the end of the session. During training sessions, participation in dyadic activities with the teacher or peer was also rated.

Reliability

Interobserver reliability measures were performed on one-third of the observations across phases of the investigation. At least two reliability checks were made during the initial baseline phase, one was during each week of training, and two were made during the follow-up probe sessions. Reliability checks were made by graduate assistants, the resource-room aide, or the teacher. Each rater independently observed the student's behavior from a 10-foot distance during a 10-minute observational period. Interobserver reliability was measured by a total reliability index (Gaylord-Ross &

Holvoet, 1985). Reliability was calculated for each behavior by dividing the smaller number of events (occurrences, seconds, or qualitative score) recorded by one observer by the larger number of events recorded by the second observer and multiplying the quotient by 100.

Mean percentage-of-agreement scores ranged from 87 percent to 100 percent across all measures. Scores for individual sessions ranged from 50 percent to 100 percent.

Overall Social Competence

Changes in self-perception and self-concept among the visually impaired students were evaluated immediately before and after training by the teacher's oral administration of the 28-item Perceived Competence Scale for Children (PCSC) (Harter, 1979) to the students. The PCSC evaluates four areas: cognitive competence, social competence, physical competence, and general self-esteem. Its psychometric reliability and validity have been established (Harter, 1982).

Social Validation

Two forms of social validation were used—the peer questionnaire and the teacher observation checklist (both of which are available from the first author on request). The perception of social competence in the targeted students was obtained from teachers and peers.

Twenty-three randomly selected sighted classmates of the visually impaired students and the five peer trainers completed the seven-item peer questionnaire on their own. They did so before the training and immediately after completion of the intervention phases. The questionnaire contains seven Likert-scale items that ask about the acceptance and liking of the targeted disabled peer.

The 15 regular education teachers completed the teacher observation checklist on their mainstreamed visually impaired students before the training and immediately following the intervention. The teachers were told to observe the students' interactive behavior during an unstructured time in the classroom or during a group activity on the playground and to rate specific social behaviors on a seven-point Likert scale.

Experimental Groups

Control Group

Observational data were collected for students who were randomly assigned to the control group across all phases of the investigation, but the students received no intervention. Each control student was paired with a student from another treatment group so the dates and frequency of observations were nearly identical. For example, if a control student was paired with a teacher-directed participant and the latter student was absent for two days, data would not be collected for the control student until the treatment student returned.

Peer-Mediated Group

The visually impaired students who were randomly assigned to the peer-mediated group received training three times a week for four weeks (12 sessions), conducted by the sighted peers. The training took place in the resource room or the playground (when it was not in use) three times a week for 40-minute sessions.

In addition, the sighted peers received weekly in-service training from the first author to structure the focus of training. At the start of every week of training, the teacher met with each pair of sighted peer trainers for 30 minutes. One student was the permanent trainer in all the sessions; the second student was a backup in case the first student was absent (although such absences never occurred). The visually impaired student was not present during these sessions. Since the sighted students had some experience with their visually impaired classmates, the teacher asked them about the student's functioning. For example, some peers were concerned that a blind student might not be able to play a game on the playground or participate in an activity without the use of vision. Other peers thought that if a student read braille, he or she had no vision. Through discussion, the students gained a more realistic perspective of their peer's abilities. (For a description of the procedures and outcomes of the in-service training sessions, see Table 2 in the appendix at the end of this chapter.)

After the training session, the first author taught the sighted students strategies to train their visually impaired peers in the first targeted behavior. The students were told which behavior would be emphasized during the week's behavioral training sessions, were asked why such behavior might be important to learn, and were given reasons why visually impaired students might have difficulty learning it. After the students role-played the behavior, they were asked: "How did you feel or what did that behavior tell you?" and "If a sighted friend did _____, what would you do?" The students' responses helped the teacher develop protocols for peer training.

When the sighted students had difficulty providing appropriate responses, the teacher modeled specific responses for them to use during training and at other times.

The behavioral training began when the sighted student entered the resource room at a designated time during the school day. The teacher would ask the sighted student and the visually impaired student, "What activity have you selected for today?" If the students were unable to agree on an activity within five minutes, the teacher gave them suggestions. (Such indecision usually occurred only during the first two days of training.) From then on, the teacher did not interact with the students for the remainder of the session and stayed at least 10 feet from the students. Although the peer-training procedures were unstructured and individualized for each visually impaired student, the sighted students consistently used the prompting statements and modeling strategies they learned during the in-service sessions. After each training session, the teacher met with the sighted student to provide positive feedback and suggestions to strengthen his or her training. Table 3 (in the appendix at the end of this chapter) describes the types of exchanges and activities that occurred during behavioral training.

Teacher-Directed Group

The visually impaired students who were randomly assigned to the teacher-directed group received structured training in social skills directed by a teacher (the first author). The instruction included modeling, verbal feedback, and role playing. As with the peer-mediated group, there were 12 sessions (three times a week for four weeks); each session lasted about 40 minutes.

Initially, the first author introduced the targeted behavior by asking the student to define and to explain the importance of the behavior in social situations. She asked questions or used prompting phrases to help the student understand the need to learn the behavior.

The teacher then modeled appropriate social responses. If the student had no usable vision, she physically guided him or her through the behavior. Next, she used role-play scenarios to practice the targeted behavior. During each practice trial, the teacher would frequently intervene by modeling appropriate verbal responses or physically demonstrating an appropriate body position or stance and by teaching alternate strategies to help the participant engage in positive social encounters. At least two role-play scenes were rehearsed during each session. After each role-play trial, the teacher provided verbal feedback about the student's performance. At the end of each session, the teacher and the student reviewed the skills the student had acquired. Similarly, at the beginning of a session, the student reviewed the skills learned for targeted social behaviors during previous sessions.

The teacher employed other strategies, such as teaching the student to rehearse typical conversational topics and phrases used by his or her sighted peers. She also used modeling and prompting to help the student incorporate this language into natural social contexts, and she introduced the student to a variety of games that his or her classmates often played.

Probe Conditions

Each visually impaired student in the three conditions was repeatedly observed in probe settings using the seven behaviors. A series of 7 to 15 baseline probes were taken. After baseline and concurrent with training, 3 to 12 generalization probes were completed. About a third of the generalization probes occurred on days when there was no training, a third occurred on the same day at least 60 minutes after training, and a third occurred at follow-up four weeks after the end of training. The seven behaviors were measured in the same probe settings for four consecutive days.

Experimental Design

A multiple-baseline design across behaviors (Kazdin, 1982) was used to evaluate the changes in social behavior in each visually impaired student. Individual data collected for one student in an experimental group was replicated with four other students. The sequence of targeted behaviors was counterbalanced across participants in each treatment condition. The individual scores were then tabulated in the three experimental groups across the four treatment conditions.

RESULTS

Behavioral Data

Peer-Mediated Training

The effects of the peer-mediated approach were consistent and positive. Figure 1 (in the appendix at the end of this chapter) displays the representative graph relating to Beth, one of the students (copies of graphs relating to all the students in the three study groups are available from the first author). On all seven dependent measures there was an increase in levels of response from the baseline to training. Consequently, Beth's social responses were elevated in the generalization probe setting. Furthermore, she was maintaining many of the social behaviors at the follow-up. These trends in the data are evident in the aggregated group mean scores.

A within-groups analysis of the five participants across the four treatment conditions for each measure was conducted, using statistical procedures developed by Marascuilo and Busk (1985). The analysis produced pairwise comparisons across the four treatments. Table 4 shows that with almost all the behaviors, there was (1) a significant increase from baseline to training, (2) a significant difference (improvement) between baseline and generalization, (3) a significant increase between baseline and follow-up, and (4) no significant difference (decline) from training to generalization or to follow-up (see the appendix at the end of this chapter.)

Thus, the statistical findings corroborate the trends of the group means and visual inspection of the individual graphs. In summary, the peer-mediated intervention led to the successful training of a set of social behaviors that, in turn, were generalized and maintained in a natural setting.

Teacher-Directed Training

The effects of the teacher-directed intervention are represented in the graph of Phil's data (see Figure 2 in the appendix at the end of this chapter). It shows that there was an increase from baseline to training in almost all the behaviors, but little or no generalization to the natural setting, since the level of social response at follow-up was similar to the response at baseline. This pattern was reflected in the graphs for the other four students. The mean scores for the five students that appear also show this pattern. The randomization test applied to this data set was identical to the one used for the peer-mediated group. The within-group, pairwise comparisons generally indicate (1) a significant increase in responding from baseline to training and (2) a significant decline in responding from training to generalization and from training to follow-up. Thus, the statistical, means, and visual analyses indicate that social responding increased in the training condition, but there was no carryover to the generalization and follow-up conditions.

Control

No individual graph is presented for the control students because there were no behavioral changes across the conditions. Mean scores for the five control participants demonstrated similar effects. When the same randomization test (which was used with the treatment groups) was applied, there were no significant differences, except for the increase ($p < .05$) from baseline to generalization for positive initiations and frequency of joining group activities. Visual inspection of the individual graphs showed that only two of the five students increased their positive initiations from baseline to generalization (but none increased the frequency of joining in group activities or in engaging any other behaviors). Thus, visual inspection does not lead to the conclusion of a significant difference for the control conditions compared to the other two treatments. According to Park, Marascuilo, and Gaylord-Ross (1987), an intervention should be considered significant in single-case data only when there is a joint agreement between the visual and statistical analyses. Such agreement was found in the peer-mediated and teacher-directed conditions, but not in the control condition.

Social Competence

The changes on the PCSC from the pretest to the posttest were evaluated across the three treatment groups. A two-sample Wilcoxon test found that the peer-mediated and teacher-directed groups had significantly larger ($p < .01$) change scores than did the control group (the peer-mediated group improved by 24 points; the teacher-directed group by 16 points; and the control group, by 4 points). Although the greatest change occurred in the peer-mediated group, no significant difference was found between it and the teacher-directed group.

Social Validation

Peer Questionnaire

The pretraining and posttraining scores on the peer questionnaire were statistically analyzed on an item-by-item basis. A matched-pair Wilcoxon test was applied within each treatment group. The control group showed no significant changes on any item from the pretest to the posttest. Both the peer-mediated and the teacher-directed groups showed significant ($p < .05$) increases on two items: "Would you choose the visually handicapped student to be your friend?" and If he [or she] "was your friend, would some of your other friends want to play with both of you?" The peer-mediated group also improved ($p < .05$) on the item, "How much would you like to play" with the visually impaired child? There were no significant changes in any of the groups on the other four items.

Teacher Observation Checklist

The pretest and posttest item scores on the teacher observation checklist were statistically analyzed for each group. According to the matched-pair Wilcoxon test, the peer-mediated group showed significant ($p < .05$) improvement on all the items except "initiations...to adult." The teacher-directed group improved only on the gaze and body-posture items. The control group showed no change on any item.

DISCUSSION

The multiple findings demonstrated the effectiveness of social-skills training for elementary-aged students with visual impairments in an integrated school setting. Generally, there were improvements in social behaviors, self-perception, peers' ratings, and teachers' ratings for the two intervention groups, but not for the control group. Upon closer examination, the changes in the peer-mediated group were superior to those in the teacher-directed group. The peer-mediated group acquired the social behaviors during training and later generalized and maintained them in a natural setting, whereas the teacher-directed group did not generalize or maintain the behaviors after training.

Of particular import, the teacher-directed group had somewhat greater gains in social behavior during training than did the peer-mediated group. That is, the teacher of the visually impaired students was somewhat superior in training targeted social behaviors than was a primary-grade sighted peer. Yet, the lack of generalization by those in the teacher-directed group is striking and worthy of further investigation.

One way in which generalization may be promoted is through the "method of common stimuli" (Stokes & Baer, 1977), which uses a stimulus in the child's natural environment that may promote or foster change. In this case, since sighted peers were present when the visually impaired student performed social behaviors both during peer-mediated training and during generalization probes, the peers could serve as common stimuli to evoke similar social responses. In contrast, there was no peer present during teacher-directed training, and the teacher did not serve as a common stimulus between the training and generalization probes.

It is also possible that the method of building natural contingencies of reinforcement into the training setting was in evidence (Stokes & Baer, 1977). Just as the peer trainers served as common discriminative stimuli, they also brought about positive consequences during training and generalization. In contrast, it is possible that the positive consequences brought about by the teacher during training were different from those of the peers in the natural setting. Certainly, further research could clarify the characteristics of consequent events between teachers and peers during training and generalization.

There may also be stylistic differences in presenting instructional stimuli. In this study, the teacher-directed method was formal in delivering antecedent stimuli, conducting behavioral rehearsal, and providing feedback on consequences. Peer-mediated training was structured more informally, so the sighted peer would induce a visually impaired student to play games and share materials. Thus, the stylistic characteristics of the peer-mediated procedure may have more in common (stimuli) with the natural-play encounters of elementary school children and thus lead to better generalization than may a teacher-directed approach.

Although the behavioral data demonstrated the superiority of the peer-mediated method, the data on social validity and social competence were less clear cut. The two treatment groups were statistically equivalent on changes in self-perception and peer ratings. Yet, the teachers thought that the peer-mediated group improved more than did the teacher-directed or control groups. It is interesting that the only item on which the teachers thought that the peer-mediated group did not show improvement was initiating interactions with adults. Since the visually impaired students did not train with adults, it is logical that they did not improve on this item. As would be expected, the peer-mediated students did improve on the initiations-with-peers item. Perhaps, because of their previous classroom experiences, the teachers were able to discriminate more accurately about changes in social behavior (see Strain & Kohler, 1988). In our anecdotal observations, there appeared to be more ostensible changes in the related and nontargeted behaviors of the peer-mediated participants. These changes in particular individuals included the following:

- Spending more time seeking peers at lunch and recess and less solitary free time in the resource room.
- Trying out for a school play.

- Being invited to a sighted peer's home after school.
- Increasing group activities with higher-status sighted peers.

Certainly, such observations are anecdotal and need to be systematically verified. Yet, they point to the types of correlated behaviors that were observed only in the peer-mediated group.

The study also points to the need for social-skills training for visually impaired students. All but 1 of the 15 students displayed low baseline levels of social behavior like eye contact (gaze), positive initiations, and ability to join and share in peer-group activities. These low levels were present even though all the students were mainstreamed in regular education classes. The study thus duplicates previous work with other groups of disabled children, such as Gaylord-Ross, Haring, Breen, and Pitts-Conway's (1984; see also, Gaylord-Ross & Pitts-Conway, 1984) study of autistic youths, which showed that mere physical integration with minimal social contact does not lead to substantive social interaction. Only with social-skills training do the rate and type of social interactions between disabled and nondisabled students increase significantly.

Although a case has been made for peer-mediated social-skills training, a number of questions still remain. We have already discussed the need for a better understanding of the components of peer-mediated training. One investigation might contrast the differential effects of the present training program with one that uses visually impaired students as trainers. If common-person (stimulus) characteristics play a role, then the similar attributes of a visually impaired trainer might enhance generalization.

Furthermore, although the successful maintenance of social behavior was demonstrated at a one-month follow-up, what about the long-term duration of social response? Since the present training program consisted of only 12 sessions, it is possible that long-term effects may be enhanced with more intensive training.

In conclusion, many research questions need to be answered to demonstrate more clearly the effectiveness of social-skills training with blind and visually impaired children. Although blind and visually impaired children have been increasingly mainstreamed in regular public schools, it has yet to be shown how they can have rewarding social interactions and avoid isolation from peers. Social-skills training is potentially useful for enhancing the educational integration and the development of social behavior in these students.

CHAPTER 6, APPENDIX

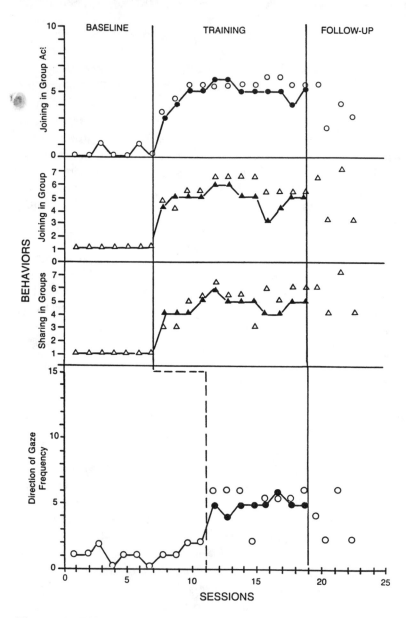

Figure 1. Effects of Peer-Mediated Social-Skills Training for Beth.

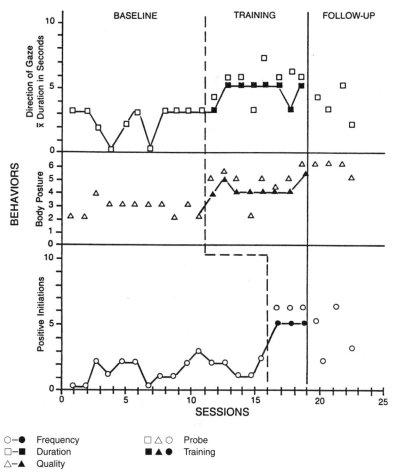

○–● Frequency   □ △ ○ Probe
□–■ Duration   ■ ▲ ● Training
△–▲ Quality

Figure 1. *continued*

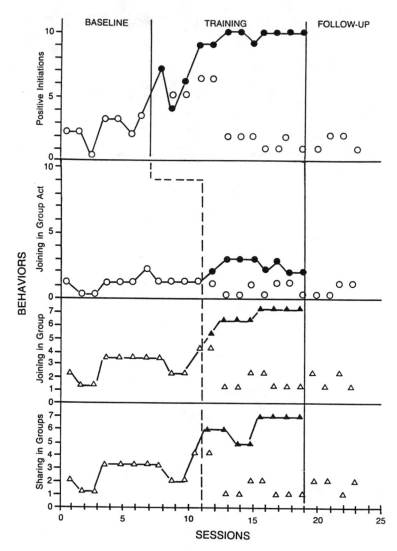

Figure 2. Effects of Teacher-Directed Social-Skills Training for Phil.

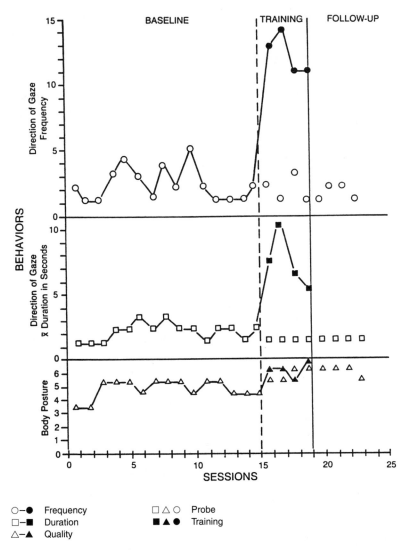

Figure 2. *continued*

Table 1. Characteristics of the Blind and Visually Impaired Students in the Three Groups

Students' Age (in years and months) and Grade	Academic Development (Teacher's Report)	Cause of Visual Impairment
PEER-MEDIATED GROUP		
Beth (8.2 years, third grade)	On grade level	Glaucoma
Eric (8.3 years, third grade)	On grade level	Optic nerve trauma
Charles 9.6 years, fourth grade)	One year below grade level	Glaucoma
Anna (11.7 years, sixth grade)	On grade level	Optic nerve tumors
Laura (7.6 years, second grade)	Six months below grade level	Albinism
TEACHER-DIRECTED GROUP		
Jason (12.2 years, sixth grade)	One year below grade level	Optic nerve hypoplasia
Robert (7.2 years, second grade)	One year below grade level	Retinopathy of prematurity
Geof (8 years, third grade)	On grade level	Albinism
Phil (8.6 years, third grade)	On grade level	Optic atrophy
Henry (11.2 years, fifth grade)	One year below grade level	Cancer of the eye
CONTROL GROUP		
Diana (11.10 years, sixth grade)	One year below grade level	Retinopathy of prematurity
Tom (11.6 years, fourth grade)	Two years below grade level	Optic nerve coloboma
Michelle (11.0 years, fourth grade)	Two years below grade level	High fever, malnutrition
Mark (12.2 years, fifth grade)	One year below grade level	Micropthalmus
Lisa (7.11 years, second grade)	On grade level	Optic nerve tumors

[1]NLP = no light perception, LP = light perception, OU = both eyes.

Table 1.
continued

Visual Acuity[1]	Main Reading Mode	Percentage of Time in Mainstream Classrooms	Initial Social Behavior
NLP(OU)	Braille	90 percent	Quiet, shy
LP(OU)	Braille	80 percent	Overly verbal, ego centered
20/400(left eye) NLP(right eye)	Print/ braille	60 percent	Passive, shy
20/400(OU)	Print	80 percent	Passive, shy
20/400(OU)	Print	80 percent	Aggressive, hostile tone
20/400(OU)	Print	30 percent	Shy, immature, friendly to adults
20/800(OU)	Print	50 percent	Quiet, shy
20/200(OU)	Print	95 percent	Assertive, has many friends
NLP(left eye) 20/200(right eye)	Braille	60 percent	Overly verbal
NLP(OU)	Braille	90 percent	Aggressive, frequently fights
NLP(OU)	Braille	30 percent	Passive, shy
20/800(left eye) NLP(right eye)	Print/ braille	50 percent	Covertly aggressive, socially integrated, has a group of friends
NLP(OU)	Braille	75 percent	Quiet, shy, has some friends
NLP(left eye) 20/400(right eye)	Print	100 percent	Aggressive, fights
20/200(OU) fluctuates	Braille	30 percent	Quiet, has friends

Table 2. In-service Training Protocols for Use with Sighted Peer Trainers

INTRODUCTION TO THE VISUALLY IMPAIRED STUDENT AND A DESCRIPTION OF HIS OR HER VISUAL IMPAIRMENT (BEHAVIOR TRAINED)

Procedure
Name and describe the specific visual disability. You may use simulation of the visual impairment to help the peers understand the adaptations and limitations incurred by the visually impaired student. Discuss the ways in which visually impaired students can adapt and participate in activities in school and community in each session. Follow the sequence of training for the peer-mediated approach and randomly select a targeted behavior for training. Answer questions and clarify any preconceived notions about how visually impaired individuals perform tasks.

Outcomes
The peer trainers will develop a heightened awareness of and sensitivity to the students' abilities and limitations and more realistic expectations of them.

DIRECTION OF GAZE (EYE CONTACT) AND BODY POSTURE (BEHAVIOR TRAINED SIMULTANEOUSLY)

Procedure
Name and define the behavior being trained. Discuss the importance of using appropriate eye contact and body posture in social situations. Have the sighted peers identify the elements of acceptable eye contact and body posture. Ask the students to interpret the meaning of specific behaviors being modeled by the investigator (for example, have the investigator talk to students but not look at them, or have the investigator keep his or her head down while engaged in a conversation). Ask the students how they would change the behaviors modeled. If the students do not respond, provide specific prompting procedures, such as verbal phrases ("Look up") or physical prompts (a tap on the shoulder). Provide role-play scenarios in which the sighted peers must employ corrective feedback or praise. Encourage the peers to praise their visually impaired counterparts, but also to give honest feedback. Use role plays that reflect experiences that both peers have encountered. Have the sighted peers practice corrective and praise responses through the role-play scenes until the desired responses are used with 80 percent proficiency.

Outcomes
The visually impaired students will improve their ability to initiate and to maintain appropriate gazes and postures in a variety of social contexts. The incidence of mannerisms (such as rocking and head or hand waving) will be reduced to enhance acceptable body posture.

POSITIVE SOCIAL INITIATIONS (BEHAVIOR TRAINED)

Procedure
Name and define the behavior being trained. Discuss with sighted peers the way they greet friends, the topics they discuss, and the games and activities they particularly like to play. Have the sighted students role-play a typical social interaction or greeting. Ask the students to analyze the good and bad parts of the interaction. Emphasize that interactions or initiations have a beginning, a middle,

Table 2. *continued*

and an end. Ask the sighted peers to think about what part of an initiation may be particularly difficult for a visually impaired student. If the sighted students have difficulty responding, you may prompt some thoughts (for example, "If you cannot see another person standing nearby, how do you know the person's identity or that there is a peer close by?") Encourage solutions, such as providing verbal feedback or using auditory cues or sensation cues (changes in temperature or shadowing). Present role plays in which you assume the role of the visually impaired student. Present situations for sighted peers in which the visually impaired student will not initiate a conversation, is overly verbal, or is overly aggressive and uses hostile phrases to engage in social interactions. Provide verbal feedback (praise or prompts) for each response by the sighted peer. Model specific responses or initiators to specific situations (for example, if the visually impaired student is overly verbal [talks about the same topic or self], have the sighted peer use phrases, such as, "You always talk about that. How about changing the subject?" or "Gee! I really like you, but I can't get a word in. You're always talking"). Encourage the sighted student to train the visually impaired student to use complimenting statements about others (such as "good shot" or "that's great"). Have the sighted peer practice phrases and statements that will prompt the visually impaired student to use initiators (for example, "Hi, How ya doin? I like what you're wearing today"), icebreakers (such as, "Wanna have lunch together? Hey, did you watch Cosby last night?"), or engaging statements (for instance, "You were great in class today. I have that Transformer"). Practice role plays until prompts and feedback responses are used with 80 percent proficiency.

Outcomes
The visually impaired students will demonstrate increased positive initiations with peers, expanded conversations, and greater use of complimenting statements.

JOINING IN GROUP ACTIVITIES (BEHAVIOR TRAINED SIMULTANEOUSLY WITH SHARING IN GROUP ACTIVITIES)

Procedure
Name and define the behavior being trained. Have the sighted students describe how they join a group on the playground at recess, in the cafeteria at lunch, or in the classroom during a free-time activity. Explain or reinforce how the effect of limited vision or no vision may influence independent joining. Blindfold or use vision simulators on the sighted students. Have the sighted students practice joining a group and engaging in play while under simulation. Have the sighted peers provide impressions and discuss ways to facilitate joining. If the sighted students do not provide solutions, offer several suggestions (such as meeting a friend at a designated spot and having the visually impaired student practice asking for assistance to find a friend or a particular game on the playground). Have the sighted students practice phrases that will help the visually impaired students gain entry to groups in a positive manner (for example, "Gee, can I play?" or, "How about playing _____?"). Use role plays and actual practice in natural settings until phrases and prompts are used with 80 percent proficiency.

Outcomes
The visually impaired students will enter group activities in an independent manner. If assistance is needed, they will use statements that generate positive responses from peers.

(continued on next page)

Table 2. *continued*

SHARING IN GROUP ACTIVITIES (BEHAVIOR TRAINED SIMULTANEOUSLY WITH JOINING IN GROUP ACTIVITIES—AN EXTENSION OF JOINING)

Procedure

Name and define the behavior being trained. Ask the sighted peers to describe both positive and negative sharing techniques. Help them understand that without sight or with limited vision, the visually impaired students may need help with turn taking in game playing or interrupting in actual conversations. Teach the sighted students phrases or statements to help the visually impaired students become aware of turn-taking techniques (for instance, "Hey, _____, just wait a minute" or, "Wait for your turn" or, "You're interrupting me, wait a minute, okay?"). Have the sighted students teach the visually impaired students games that will facilitate sharing and turn taking (such as, "It's just a game" or, "You don't always have to win" or, "Don't get so upset, it's only a game"). Provide role-play situations in which the sighted students can practice corrective responses and honest feedback with 80 percent proficiency.

Outcomes

The visually impaired students will increase their ability to share in a variety of group situations using turn-taking techniques and asserting their rights in a positive manner.

Table 3. Peer-Mediated Training Activities, Interactions, and Responses among Sighted Peers to Visually Impaired Students for Each Targeted Behavior

Behavior	Activities	Input from Sighted Peers	Responses of Visually Impaired Students
Direction of Gaze and Body Posture	Board games (Checkers, Simon, Sorry, Connect Four, Monopoly, Fish, 21, Othello), computer games, outdoor games, playing on equipment (play structure), hand claps, and finger plays	Phrases used: "Hey! Sit up". "_____, when you talk to me, how about looking at me?" "_____ [pause]." "_____, you look really neat." "_____, please stop that."	Verbal responses: "Okay, I forgot." "Thanks for reminding me." "Ya, I'll stop." "Ya, I know I do." Nonverbal responses: sits or stands with appropriate posture and longer gaze
Positive Initiations	Drawing on blackboard; playing with dolls, a dollhouse, Transformers, or action figures; sharing a snack or toy; talking about school	"Gee, you did a good job." "What do you want to play? You decide." "Hi! What's new? What did you watch last night? So, what's happening?" "It would sure be great if you could come over after school." "Hey, did you hear about _____? He likes _____."	"Ya, thanks, it's a _____." "How about dolls or a game?" "Hi, how ya doin? Hey, did you see Alf last night?" "I'd like that, but I have to ask my mom, and figure a way home." "No, what happened? He's cute."

(continued on next page)

Table 3. continued

Behavior	Activities	Input from Sighted Peers	Responses of Visually Impaired Students
Joining in Group Activities	Playing on play equipment (dramatic play), kickball, wallball, basketball, chase, jump rope	"Okay, ———, let's meet and then we can play ———." "Wanta play kickball?" [peer runs off] "Okay, ———, it's your turn."	"I'll meet you at the drinking fountain." "Ya, wait for me." "Thanks, but where do I stand?"
Joining in Activities and Sharing in Group Activities	Dramatic play with action figures, waiting in line for food in the cafeteria, eating lunch on the grass (small group), hanging out on a bench (conversing), walking around the play area, indoor activities (cooking projects, computer games, puzzles, "hangman," board games, art projects)	"Just wait, ———, I'll go after you, all right? It's ——— turn." "First you'll have a turn, and then me."	"Okay, I'll wait." "That sounds great."

Table 4. Randomization Test Statistics for the Within-Group Comparisons Across Each Dependent Measure for the Peer-Mediated Intervention

Dependent Measure	Baseline	Training	Generalization Probe
DURATION OF GAZE			
Training	2.17		
Generalization probe	3.46**		
Follow-up probe	2.07	–0.10	–1.39
FREQUENCY OF GAZE			
Training	2.50*		
Generalization probe	3.56**	1.05	
Follow-up probe	3.14**	.64	–0.42
BODY POSTURE			
Training	1.93		
Generalization probe	3.30**	1.31	
Follow-up probe	3.78**	1.79	.48
POSITIVE INITIATIONS			
Training	2.98**		
Generalization probe	4.07**	1.09	
Follow-up probe	3.18**	.20	–0.89
FREQUENCY OF JOINING IN GROUP ACTIVITIES			
Training	2.59*		
Generalization probe	4.00**	1.41	
Follow-up probe	2.54*	–0.04	–1.45
QUALITY OF JOINING IN GROUP ACTIVITIES			
Training	2.64*		
Generalization probe	3.32**	.68	
Follow-up probe	3.92**	1.27	.59
QUALITY OF SHARING IN GROUP ACTIVITIES			
Training	2.80*		
Generalization probe	3.52**	.72	
Follow-up probe	3.78**	.99	.27

* Significant for the family of planned pairwise comparisons when the overall error rate is controlled at alpha = .05 for a one-tailed test when z > 2.39.

** Significant for the family of planned pairwise comparisons when the overall error rate is controlled at alpha = .01 for a one-tailed test when z > 2.39.

Part 3: Strategies for Educators and Implications for Further Research

Thus far, this volume has established a strong theoretical and research knowledge base to justify and demonstrate the importance of social-skills interventions for students with visual impairments. It should be noted, however, that the research is a foundation for additional investigations by teachers and other professionals. The reader should not assume that the applied strategies presented in the research section are the culmination of social-skills research. Rather, these methodologies are meant to be expanded within creative research endeavors as well as in practical educational and living environments.

Practice is derived from theory and research. The chapters that follow are intended to help professionals and parents implement individualized social-skills training activities in real settings. The suggestions presented here can be used for a range of activities to meet the diverse needs of blind and visually impaired students of various ages and in various grades and educational placements. The strategies should neither be considered as encyclopedic nor used as "recipes." Rather, the ideas presented are meant to allow professionals to design and to modify creative interventions that, in essence, will facilitate social growth for the student and for his or her peers.

Strategies must be designed with the individual student in mind. Assessments based on observations of the student's social competence in natural contexts can assist the teacher of visually impaired students, the regular education teacher, and family members in determining programs to maximize social integration. This form of assessment allows the teachers to monitor a student's behavior in a variety of situations throughout the school year. It also allows the teachers and the parents to become acquainted with the sighted peer culture and its many nuances. As adults, we can learn a great deal about the social world of children through observation. For example, we can learn what lingo is current and what is not or how the rules of a game like Four Square are initiated and carried out. By acquainting ourselves with the culture and social world of children and youths, we can facilitate the greater inclusion of students with visual impairments.

In Chapter 7, Sacks and Kekelis present a range of recommendations (derived from their qualitative study presented in Chapter 4) to help teachers and parents promote social contacts with sighted peers. These recommendations center on the following topics: classroom placements and environments, ongoing in-service training for peers and teachers, friendship-making skills, the use of adults as aides in the regular education classroom, and peers as helpers and agents of social change in the classroom. Each group of recommendations is delineated for teachers of visually impaired students, regular education teachers, and parents.

More specific strategies for social-skills training are presented in Chapter 8. In that chapter, Sacks and Reardon provide numerous examples of interventions that can be infused into the academic curriculum or directly initiated with blind and visually impaired students in the school or in the community. Specific lesson plans to assist teachers in designing their own programs are included, as are examples of how commercially produced curricula can be adapted and used with students with visual impairments. In addition, suggestions for parents and professionals regarding instruction concerning eye contact, personal space, physical and facial gestures, and nonverbal communication are presented, and the importance of including visually impaired students in all aspects of decision making is emphasized.

One highly successful way to promote social integration of children is through play. However, when students with visual impairments spend time in free-play situations such as recess, they are often at a disadvantage and may feel isolated. Orienting oneself to an open, unstructured playground or quad area to facilitate social contacts with peers is a challenge for many visually impaired students. In a pilot study, Macks became keenly aware of the need for teachers, peers, and parents to introduce activities that all students, visually impaired or sighted, could participate in with equal levels of success. In Chapter 9, she describes a number of games that promote group interaction and social inclusion for visually impaired students and demonstrates how peers can promote and manipulate positive social experiences for their visually impaired counterparts when teachers include them in the implementation process.

This section would not be complete without the contributions of Pogrund and Strauss in Chapter 10. This article, previously published by the American Foundation for the Blind in the *Journal of Visual Impairment & Blindness*, is fundamental to the discipline of social-skills training for students with visual impairments. When one evaluates social competence in a visually impaired student, it is a given that the student needs to acquire and to maintain a high level of self-esteem and social identity. Sally Mangold, in "Nurturing High Self-Esteem in Visually Handicapped Children" (1980), provided the basis for understanding how positive self-esteem influences the development of social competence among students with visual impairments.

Pogrund and Strauss enhance the strategies set forth by Mangold by presenting a number of activities that promote assertive behavior and positive social communication skills among visually impaired individuals. The premise behind these activities is that the acquisition of assertiveness skills will promote visually impaired students' independent living and increase their decision-making abilities. The activities presented can be easily incorporated by teachers or family members on an ongoing basis. In addition, they are created so that students can talk freely about their feelings and identities as visually impaired persons. Many of the activities promote group interaction through role playing or board games. Other activities can be done on an individual basis by using journal writing or sentence completion to facilitate or encourage discussion. Finally, the use of these strategies with sighted peers or colleagues can further promote social integration.

The underlying intent of this section is to stimulate the reader and to serve as a springboard for the implementation of further social-skills activities between visually impaired persons and their peers, colleagues, and family members. Teachers and parents can develop their own strategies on the basis of their own observations of a child. It is hoped that the strategies presented here will be applied in a range of educational, home, and community settings. By stimulating social awareness in our students, we can foster a sense of independence and empowerment—the true goal of education and rehabilitation.

Chapter 7

Guidelines for Mainstreaming Blind and Visually Impaired Children

Sharon Zell Sacks and Linda S. Kekelis

The guidelines presented in this chapter were designed to assist teachers of visually impaired students, regular education teachers, and parents in mainstreaming visually impaired students into school and community environments effectively, so that the outcomes will be positive. The accompanying illustrations and suggestions are the direct result of observations and findings from our study of mainstreaming (Kekelis & Sacks, 1988), reported in Chapter 4. The guidelines address issues related to the appropriate placement of visually impaired students; the selection of appropriate materials, activities, and settings; and the understanding of the students' visual impairments. Each section delineates specific factors that contribute to the successful integration of visually impaired students and presents illustrations and suggestions to provide a framework for the inclusion of effective socialization strategies for visually impaired students and their sighted age-mates.

APPROPRIATE PLACEMENT

Although a classroom teacher's willingness to accept a visually impaired child into his or her classroom is an important consideration, it is not sufficient for a successful mainstreaming experience. Each of the six children discussed in Chapter 4 was placed with a teacher who had agreed to work with a visually impaired child, yet the teachers differed in their abilities to provide a positive experience for the students. Therefore, a number of factors need to be considered before visually impaired children are placed in regular education classes. These factors include (1) the classroom teacher's philosophy and style of instruction, (2) the involvement of the teacher of the visually impaired student in the mainstreaming effort and the classroom teacher's willingness to request and accept support from the teacher of the visually impaired student, (3) the classroom teacher's interest in the *social*, as well as academic, development of his or her students, and (4) the social milieu of the classroom in which the visually impaired student is placed.

Guideline: The classroom teacher's philosophy and style of instruction affects the academic and social gains made by students, particularly those students who rely on the input of others to acquire skills that are generally learned through observation and modeling.

Children with visual impairments cannot acquire academic and social competence in the same manner as do their sighted peers. Therefore, learning tasks must be clearly defined and demonstrated, and teachers must give the children considerable feedback on their performance. If a regular education teacher uses a nondirective approach to work with his or her students, it is imperative that he or she understand the impact of a visual impairment on a young child's ability to learn both academic and social lessons and be willing to take a more active role in working with the visually impaired student. Even when a child's vision loss seems minimal by clinical criteria, it often requires considerable involvement by the regular education teacher.

Illustration

In our study, Bruce's kindergarten experience illustrated the negative outcome of placing a visually impaired child with a teacher who believed that young children do best when left to learn on their own. In keeping with a laissez-faire approach to learning, Bruce's teacher did little to structure her students' play and academic lessons. Without adequate guidance and supervision, Bruce's classmates displayed disruptive and aggressive behavior toward one another and failed to master many of the basic academic and social skills that are prerequisites for the first grade. For many of the students, the effects of this kindergarten experience were compensated for in first grade. For some students, however, the effects were more serious. The self-esteem of these students was threatened, and their relationships with classmates were seriously harmed. In regard to Bruce, the kindergarten experience jeopardized his educational future.

Suggestions for Regular Education Teachers and Teachers of Visually Impaired Students

- Provide a regular education experience that is structured and organized, so the visually impaired student knows what to expect.
- Create seating arrangements that enhance social experiences for the visually impaired student. For example, grouping four to six students in cooperative learning groups may assist the visually impaired student to gain entry to the peer group.
- Change seating assignments regularly so the visually impaired student has an opportunity to meet a wide range of classmates.
- Provide opportunities for the visually impaired child to select partners for group or free-play activities.

Guideline: The involvement of a teacher of a visually impaired students in education, both in the regular classroom and the resource room, has a significant impact on the success of the child's mainstreaming experience.

It is not sufficient for a visually impaired student to receive support only in the resource room or on an itinerant basis to meet academic goals set by the Individualized Education Program. Assistance from a teacher of visually impaired students must carry over to the regular education classroom and the playground.

It is important that a teacher of visually impaired students begin working toward an optimal mainstreaming experience before the student enters the regular classroom. By discussing with the classroom teacher the ways in which a student's visual impairment is likely to affect interactions with classmates and recommending ways to educate students about their classmate's visual impairment, the teacher of visually impaired students can increase the likelihood that the mainstreaming endeavor will get off to a positive start. It is critical that this teacher periodically observes the visually impaired student in the mainstream environment to assess accurately the student's social needs, which will change throughout the school year. He or she can then develop and, if possible, help implement strategies to increase positive social interactions between the visually impaired student and his or her sighted classmates.

Illustration

In our mainstreaming study, we found that the degree to which teacher of the visually impaired students was involved in the regular education classroom had a profound effect on the visually impaired students' social development and acceptance by classmates. All the resource-room teachers in our study had years of experience providing direct services to visually impaired students and knew how to support classroom teachers. However, few fully involved themselves in their students' interactions in the regular classrooms.

Suggestions for Teachers of Visually Impaired Students

- Develop effective communication styles with regular education teachers by creating an atmosphere in which questions can be answered and concerns can be discussed.

- Observe and participate in the regular education classroom on an ongoing basis.

- Create in-service training that is easy to understand. Provide ways for the regular education students to participate in simulations of vision loss and adaptive materials.

- Provide opportunities for the regular education students and regular education teacher to ask questions about the visually impaired student's visual status.

- Meet regularly with students and teachers to answer questions.

- Create opportunities for the visually impaired student to become involved in the in-service process. Help the visually impaired student to communicate his or her special needs effectively.

Guideline: In addition to academic success, the mainstreaming of visually impaired children must be evaluated against social criteria.

A regular education classroom is the least restrictive environment for a visually impaired child only if he or she participates in interactions in the classroom and the playground, is accepted by classmates, and has the opportunity to develop relationships with peers from which to learn appropriate social behavior. To achieve social goals, classroom teachers (special education and regular education) should consider a number of evaluative questions. These questions are posed throughout the following discussion.

1. Does the visually impaired student play with and talk to peers as much as do his or her classmates?

Some visually impaired children prefer the company and attention of adults. However, only by interacting with sighted classmates can they develop the social skills that are necessary for acceptance by their peer group. These children need to be encouraged to seek the company of children. They should be praised when they make an effort to talk and play with classmates; encouraged to direct comments, questions, and requests for help to peers instead of adults; and given less reinforcement when they interact with adults or play by themselves.

Illustration

In our study, we observed that when the visually impaired students were taught in the regular classroom, an instructional aide or classroom teacher would accompany the student. Often, instruction was provided in a tutorial fashion, away from the milieu of the other students. When the teacher or aide included sighted students, along with the visually impaired student, in the instructional process, the outcome was far more favorable.

Suggestions for Regular Education Teachers and Teachers of Visually Impaired Students

- Assist the visually impaired student to establish a buddy system in the classroom, at lunch, and during recess whereby the visually impaired student assumes and orchestrates the responsibility of selecting a peer.

- Provide opportunities within the regular classroom or resource room for the visually impaired student to invite a friend or small group of friends to work on a project, play a board game, or master a computer game.

- Design activities that promote cooperation and sharing between visually impaired and sighted students.

- When an aide or teacher of visually impaired students works with his or her student in the regular classroom, develop lessons and activities that include sighted classmates.

- Create activities in the regular education environment that do not isolate the visually impaired student.

2. Do students talk with their visually impaired classmates in the classroom, play with them on the playground, and invite them to after-school and weekend activities?

It is important that visually impaired children have opportunities to interact with their sighted classmates. Because the activities performed in the classroom and the playground differ, the visually impaired children should participate in both contexts.

Friendships are developed not only during school time, but after school and on weekends in the homes of children. Even when children seem to enjoy the company of a visually impaired classmate at school, they may be reluctant to invite the child to their homes. The classroom teacher can talk with the parents of the sighted students and suggest that they arrange for the visually impaired child to visit their homes. It is important that the teacher work with both families of the children who display a preference for one another to ensure a positive experience. When after-school visits from visually impaired children are forced on disinterested or even frightened classmates, the results may be negative (Kekelis, 1988a).

Illustration

In our study, we observed that the visually impaired students had few opportunities to interact with their sighted counterparts outside school because they lived far from the schools they attended. When their parents were willing to transport them for extracurricular activities (scouting, participating in drama groups, or spending time with sighted peers), their social contacts were more successful. For example, when Karen's teacher encouraged her parents to allow Karen to attend classmates' birthday parties and sleepovers, Karen's social encounters during the school day increased.

Suggestions for Parents and Teachers of Visually Impaired Students

- Encourage the parents of visually impaired students to invite sighted classmates to their homes for birthday parties, overnight stays, family outings, shopping trips, and concerts or plays.

- Provide opportunities for visually impaired students to become involved in a wide range of leisure activities. Help students to learn the "in" games (such as Nintendo and My Little Pony), the "in" language, and the "in" styles (such as tight pants and baggy sweatshirts). Also, providing students with opportunities to participate in team or group recreational activities (gymnastics, goal ball, beep baseball, roller skating, or swimming) can help initiate positive peer relationships while teaching critical social behaviors, such as sharing, turn taking, and assertive communication.

- Work with the regular education teacher to create opportunities for the parents of regular education students to become familiar with the program serving visually impaired students, as well as the students served in the program.

3. Does the visually impaired child show affection and display preference for classmates?

Children develop relationships with classmates that are mutually reinforcing. They greet one another at the start of the school day, discuss family outings after weekend separations, request and provide assistance to fellow classmates, and express feelings through facial expressions and smiles.

Illustration

Most of the visually impaired children in our study required an adult's guidance to learn how to initiate and to maintain friendships with classmates. Lee, for example, was fortunate to have input from his resource-room teacher and his regular education teacher, who spent time helping him acquire specific play skills with specific toys. Both teachers demonstrated and modeled to Lee the use and function of a range of toys and games. Through practice, Lee gained the confidence and competence to engage his sighted classmates in creative play.

Suggestions for Regular Education Teachers and Teachers of Visually Impaired Students

- Identify classmates whom the visually impaired student prefers.

- Encourage the visually impaired student to express positive feelings toward his or her classmates.

- Encourage the visually impaired student to choose a partner for play or academic tasks, share materials and toys with classmates, and help a prospective friend accomplish an assignment.

- Encourage the visually impaired student to help his or her sighted peers.

- Facilitate discussions about friendship with the visually impaired student to help him or her become more aware of the feelings of others.

- Encourage the visually impaired student to communicate his or her visual needs to others in a simple, straightforward manner.

4. As an educator, do you observe interactions during recess, and intervene, when necessary, so the visually impaired student is not isolated on the playground?

For many classroom teachers, recess is a time to prepare lessons or to take a break. During that time, however, students play on their own under adult supervision that ensures their safety but not their involvement with classmates. Most of the visually impaired children in our study needed a great deal of support during recess if they were to participate in activities with their classmates. Although it may not be possible for a classroom teacher to accompany a visually impaired child to the playground, it is advisable that the teacher periodically monitor recess activities to keep abreast of the visually impaired student's social life outside the classroom. In some instances, a visually impaired child's isolation on the playground may be lessened with minimal involvement by the classroom teacher.

Suggestions for the Teacher of Visually Impaired Students

- Suggest games (such as Simon Says) that the visually impaired child can participate in with classmates.

- Adapt games so the visually impaired child can play with classmates. For example, provide a Beeper Ball, so the visually impaired child can play catch.

- Assign a special friend to play with the visually impaired child during recess, or have the visually impaired student choose a favorite peer.

- Provide toys for the visually impaired student to use during recess—toys that are likely to attract the interest of classmates and facilitate cooperative play—such as hand-held video games, electronic cars, "Micro machines," and action figures.

- Provide opportunities for the visually impaired student to develop skills and practice with a cadre of games and activities.

5. How does the status of the visually impaired student among his or her sighted classmates change during the school year, and how do the interactions between the visually impaired child and the sighted classmates develop?

Since the social hierarchy of a classroom is in constant flux, the classroom teacher must regularly monitor changes in the quality of social interactions between the visually impaired student and his or her sighted classmates and in the acceptance of the visually impaired student by his or her classmates. Developments that must be attended to include a decrease in the frequency with which the visually impaired child plays and converses with classmates, an increase in negative comments about the visually impaired student, the reluctance of sighted classmates to assist the visually impaired student, a decline in friendships between the visually impaired child and the sighted classmates, and no change in the play and conversations of the visually impaired student and his or her classmates.

After their initial curiosity and interest wane, the sighted classmates may ignore the visually impaired student. Visual information plays such a critical role in the conversations and play of children that a visually impaired child may not provide sufficient reinforcement to maintain relationships with sighted classmates. Even when socially skilled, the visually impaired child may get locked into stereotyped interactions with sighted classmates, who do not know how to interact without using visual cues. For visually impaired children who lack basic social skills, the consequences may be even more serious: Sighted classmates may respond with aggressive behavior. Under these circumstances, the classroom teacher must work with both the visually impaired student and the sighted classmates to facilitate interactions that are both enjoyable and rewarding for the students.

Illustration

Bruce's interactions with his classmates deteriorated over time because the children were confused about his visual abilities. Although Bruce has good residual vision, playing board games and putting puzzles together required close viewing. Bruce's peers were confused and frustrated. They accused him of cheating because he moved a games piece incorrectly. They had no understanding of Bruce's visual needs.

Suggestions for the Regular Education Teacher and Teacher of Visually Impaired Students

- Give the sighted students clear information about a student's visual status.

- Help the sighted students find alternative ways of implementing a visual activity. Allow the students to develop solutions.

- Provide opportunities for the classroom educator and the teacher of visually impaired students to brainstorm the implementation of innovative modes of instruction or activities, especially in social activities, to maximize the inclusion of the visually impaired student.

- Allow the regular education teacher to communicate feelings of both frustration and satisfaction in serving a visually impaired student. Provide solutions to problems that may arise.

Guideline: It is critical that the classroom environment in which the visually impaired student is placed promotes the social well-being of all students and encourages altruistic behavior among classmates.

Illustration

The success of Lee's mainstreaming experience and the failure of Bruce's were due, in part, to the social milieu of their kindergartens. In Lee's class, children were encouraged to show regard for the feelings of classmates, were praised when they demonstrated prosocial behavior, and were criticized for aggressive and selfish behavior. The children were given opportunities to get to know their classmates. When problems arose, Lee's teacher asked the students to reflect on their behavior and on its impact on classmates. These discussions were just as likely to benefit Lee as they were his classmates.

During academic lessons and circle time in Lee's kindergarten, seat assignments were changed regularly, so the students had opportunities to become acquainted with their classmates. This strategy encouraged the development of friendships among boys and girls and among children of different races and levels of ability. It was particularly helpful to Lee because it enabled him to become better acquainted with many of his classmates. As some classmates got to know Lee, their fears and prejudices diminished. Furthermore, several of the friendships he developed were with girls, which probably would not have occurred if assigned seating had not encouraged interactions between boys and girls.

In Bruce's class, the classroom teacher often reinforced the antisocial behavior of students. She became involved in her students' affairs when the children verbally or physically assaulted one another. She made few attempts to encourage new friendships or to promote helping behavior. The children formed cliques and incessantly argued over possessions and physical boundaries. They directed their energies toward excluding, rather than including, classmates in their play. In this environment, Bruce played and talked with only a few boys in his class and seldom played with any girls.

Suggestions for the Teacher of Visually Impaired Students

- Attempt to find placements in classrooms in which affective education is emphasized for *all* students.

- Look for regular education settings in which the classroom teacher encourages activities that promote positive self-esteem.

- At the primary level, select classroom environments in which academic performance and social competence are equally important.

- Create opportunities in the regular classroom or resource room in which the educational team can facilitate discussions of the physical, social, or emotional differences between the visually impaired student and his or her sighted peers in a relaxed, free-flowing manner.

- Help both the visually impaired and the sighted students become sensitive to the strengths and limitations of all classmates through discussions, curricular activities, or lessons on literature, language arts, and social studies in which the subject is incorporated.

SELECTION OF MATERIALS, ACTIVITIES, AND SETTINGS

The toys and materials that are available to students in the classroom and playground, along with the activities that are scheduled, significantly affect the social experiences of visually impaired children in mainstream programs.

Illustrations

Through observations, we learned that how the regular education teacher introduces, monitors, and affects change in negative play situations has a critical impact on the successful inclusion of the visually impaired student into the integrated classroom. The illustrations provided in this section include examples of activities that yielded positive social outcomes for the visually impaired students in our study.

Multipiece Toys

In the classroom, multipiece toys, such as Lincoln Logs, blocks, and Legos, promoted conversations and cooperative play between the visually impaired student and the sighted classmates. These toys, which were used in a confined area on floors or on tables, made it possible for children with severe visual impairments to monitor the whereabouts of playmates and play materials. During play with these materials, conversations focused on the children's constructions. In addition, the open-ended nature of play with such materials enabled the visually impaired children to produce creations that were considered to be just as good as or better than the creations of their sighted classmates.

Artwork

Painting also facilitated conversations between visually impaired children and their sighted classmates. Because the activity was open ended, the visually impaired student could experiment with mixing colors, use paint brushes, and work on his or her painting without assistance from a teacher or from classmates. This is an important consideration when choosing activities for visually impaired children because the presence of an adult, no matter how well meaning, often interferes with peer interactions and shifts the focus of conversations from child- to adult-directed topics.

The finished paintings of the visually impaired students did not look much different from those of their classmates. For most other art activities, this was not the case. We found, for example, that drawing with pencils and crayons did not work as well as did painting. Pencils and crayons were generally used to achieve more specific goals, such as drawing a Christmas tree for the holiday season or a groundhog on Groundhog Day.

To accomplish these goals, a visually impaired student requires considerable assistance from an adult or a classmate. During our investigation, we observed that when visually impaired children asked their peers for help with drawings, they often interfered with their classmates' work. When they sought the assistance of a teacher, the art project ceased to be an opportunity for peer interactions. Even with assistance, the completed artwork of visually impaired students looked different from their classmates' work and seemed to accentuate the limitations imposed by the impairment. However, when the visually impaired child was allowed to team with a sighted classmate to complete an art project, the end result was a truly combined effort. It is important to keep in mind that the teacher needs to select a peer who will encourage equal participation. Experiences with such peers can help the visually impaired student share responsibility for the completion of a task, learn to cooperate and work with others, and assist others when help is needed, instead of always asking for assistance.

Board Games

The success of board games among kindergarten and first-grade students (visually impaired or sighted) depends upon the classroom teacher's ability to plan and monitor the students' participation in the games. It is important that the visually impaired student fully understands the concept of the game and that ample time is provided for the child to explore the game. Once the visually impaired student has mastered the rules of the game, the classroom teacher should select appropriate partners for the child, who can clarify rules, allow the visually impaired child longer turns, and negotiate conflicts. It is the teacher's responsibility to identify students who could benefit most from playing games with their visually impaired classmate and who could provide a positive play experience for the visually impaired child. With proper supervision, visually impaired students can participate equally in board games that are popular among their classmates—games that are played among friends outside school. These activities provide opportunities for children to learn rules for turn taking, resolving conflicts, and cooperating with peers and to develop perspective-taking and helping skills.

Playing House

A designated area for playing house can provide a setting in which visually impaired children may display their social skills. Familiar household objects, a confined space, clearly defined roles, and a limited number of playmates make it easier for visually impaired children to play with their sighted peers. The classroom teacher should carefully observe the students' play to make certain that the visually impaired child is allowed to practice roles of different status, that is, to be both a doctor and a patient, a parent and a child, a teacher and a student. Because it is easier for the child to interact with competent adults, it is critical that the teacher make his or her observations in an unobtrusive manner.

Although the rules for free-play periods vary from classroom to classroom, it is important that playhouse activities in less structured classes are governed by some regulations. When children are allowed to choose their activities and can come and go as they please, it may be difficult for the visually impaired student to monitor the arrivals and departures of others and impossible for him or her to participate in any meaningful role playing or pretend play.

Recess

Outside the classroom, the choice of toys and activities is even more critical for the visually impaired student's social experience. The unstructured nature of recess activities, the lack of toys in the playground, the rate of change in activities, and the extended physical boundaries of playgrounds may limit a visually impaired child's opportunities to participate in activities with peers. During outdoor recess, visually impaired children—even those who are socially skilled—may have difficulty displaying their underlying competence in carrying on conversations and participating in games with their sighted peers. Because staff are often only minimally involved in recess periods, negative peer interactions may go unnoticed or be left unaltered if they are noticed. Providing specific activities, such as jumping rope, four square, tether ball, and water or sand play, helps to extend the time children will engage in a social encounter with each other.

Toys and activities should be selected on an individual basis, depending on the visually impaired child's interests and skills. At one of the schools in which we observed (Kekelis, 1988b), an activity table with a variety of toys was set up on the sidelines of the playground. The toys, which included water toys, Tinker Toys, cars and trucks, and space vehicles, were alternated to retain the children's interest. After the introduction of the activity table, both the amount and the quality of interactions between the visually impaired child and the sighted classmates improved. The advantage of this type of intervention is that it requires minimal involvement of a classroom teacher. However, it was used with a visually impaired child who was highly socially competent. For visually impaired children who are deficient in play skills, it may be necessary to supplement the activity table with a program in social-skills training and greater participation by the classroom teacher and teacher of visually impaired students.

Suggestions for Parents and Teachers of Visually Impaired Students

- Spend instructional time with the visually impaired student, introducing him or her to age-appropriate toys, games, and activities.

- Allow the visually impaired student to have hands-on experiences with toys, games, and activities in the home, school, and community, so there is transference from what is heard or explained (for example, in commercials on television) to the actual manipulation of the toys or game pieces.

- Provide community experiences or activities to enhance and expand conversational skills.

- Facilitate pretend play, through problem-solving activities, role playing, or group play, in a comfortable setting (such as in the home or resource room).

- Orient the visually impaired student to the toys, games, and activities available in the regular classroom.

- Reorient the visually impaired student when new toys or games are available or when the layout of the classroom changes.

- Provide structured games or activities on the playground that facilitate social interaction between the visually impaired student and his or her sighted peers.

- Find toys, games, and activities that will entice sighted peers to engage in play activities with the visually impaired child.

- Work with the visually impaired child, through role playing and modeling, to exhibit age-appropriate conversational skills and play behavior.

- Encourage the visually impaired student to invite sighted peers to play and to share prized possessions with them.

- Encourage complimenting behaviors toward other peers in play encounters.

UNDERSTANDING OF VISUAL IMPAIRMENT

After the visually impaired student is integrated into a regular classroom, it is important that the child's impairment be discussed with the sighted students as the need arises. Such discussions help sighted children understand why their visually impaired classmate may do tasks differently and, in some instances, less competently than may other students; they may also encourage students to support their visually impaired classmate, especially one with low vision, in an appropriate manner. When a child with low vision can do many of the same things as his or her sighted peers, teachers and classmates often forget the effort that is required for the child to perform certain academic and social tasks. When expectations are unrealistic and behavior is misunderstood, both the visually impaired student and others may perceive the child to be incompetent or less adequate or may assume the student has a behavioral problem. To ensure success, it is critical that ongoing communication between the visually impaired student, his or her classmates, the regular education teacher, and the teacher of visually impaired students occurs. In addition, the visually impaired student needs to develop skills that ultimately will enhance his or her ability to advocate for himself or herself.

Suggestions for Parents and Teachers of Visually Impaired Students

- Through role playing and modeling, help the visually impaired student to communicate his or her visual abilities and needs to others.

- Help the visually impaired student understand his or her visual impairment. Explain the etiology and the implications of the impairment.
- Work with family members to clarify and to define the student's visual impairment.
- Develop curricular modules to assist visually impaired students and their families to assume responsibility and advocacy for the students' visual needs (Roessing, 1983).
- Design visual-awareness activities to help sighted peers become more sensitive to the needs of their visually impaired classmates.

CONCLUSION

The guidelines presented here can be used to promote positive social exchanges between visually impaired children and their classmates in mainstream school programs, in the neighborhood, and in the community. It is important that the guidelines be tailored to meet the unique needs of each student and each educational setting. The suggestions have been provided to help parents and teachers achieve an exciting, integrated experience for both visually impaired and sighted students. They are a foundation from which new ideas and approaches can be implemented and encouraged so that a mainstream classroom can be the most appropriate placement for a visually impaired child.

Chapter 8

Maximizing Social Integration for Visually Impaired Students: Applications and Practice

Sharon Zell Sacks and Maureen P. Reardon

The acquisition of social skills is vital to the visually impaired child, who lives in a world of social interactions that are largely visually cued and expressed nonverbally. When teachers of visually impaired students help students to acquire skills, learn behaviors, and compensate for not being able to see some of the visual, observable interactions most people take for granted, they have furthered integration at its most basic level. The ability to function socially underlies every classroom or program placement and affects the quality of students' interactions in the community at large. No philosophy of services for visually impaired persons is complete if it encompasses only academic needs. The functional needs, particularly the social needs, of visually impaired children must be addressed in every setting by all those who are involved in the children's daily programs.

The program models described here present specialized opportunities for instruction in social skills. First, the teacher of visually impaired students must recognize the need for such instruction and work with the family and the student to create or support expectations of socially appropriate behavior in all areas of life. Second, within each model, the teacher can learn to recognize or create opportunities for social-skills instruction for both special education and regular education students. The role of the teacher requires flexibility. Parents, educational supervisors, and school personnel can use the teacher as a resource most effectively when traditional expectations are evaluated in light of students' needs and long-term potential. In fact, the needs of many visually impaired students who are classified as "higher" functioning may be similar to those of students with multiple disabilities. Each student needs to demonstrate a set of socially requisite behaviors to be accepted by adults and peers. This chapter presents creative and practical strategies to enhance and encourage the social integration of visually impaired students in school, at home, and in the community and, in turn, to ensure that programming for the transition from school to work is effective.

ACTIVITIES FOR SOCIAL INTEGRATION

The activities described in the discussion that follows address social-skills instruction in a wide variety of settings. We have used the activities successfully, offering them in a variety of program models. In addition, we have found that many materials that were developed commercially or by local school districts can be adapted for use with visually impaired students. They can also provide a springboard from which instructional programs can begin. For example, "Project Esteem" (Santa Clara Unified School District) contains a series of award certificates and behavioral-management materials that can easily be enlarged or brailled. "Developing an Understanding of Self and Others" (Dinkmeyer, 1970), "Magic Circle" (Ball, 1974), and "Tell It Like It Is With the Ungame" (The Ungame Co., 1975) provide meaningful ways to facilitate social interactions in group situations, both within special day classes using "reverse mainstreaming" techniques or in a mainstream classroom in which sighted and visually impaired students can learn more about one another. In addition, the professional workshops on teaching children and adults about sexuality and social interaction sponsored by the Sex and Disability Unit of the Department of Psychiatry, University of California Medical Center, San Francisco, provided the initial foundation for the development of many social-skills activities that we have implemented.

It is important to note that the opportunities for social-skills instruction are limited not by the program model or by what is readily available but, rather, by the ability of teachers and parents to identify goals based on realistic expectations for individual children and later by the students themselves. When teachers are allowed to be flexible and are given support, they can devise creative and meaningful strategies. The instructional activities presented in the following section help promote and maximize social integration among visually impaired students.

A KITCHEN CURRICULUM FOR PARENTS

Naughton and Sacks (1977) designed a curriculum to help parents of visually impaired children create activities that foster social competence, responsibility, and independence and that enhance cognitive and language skills through experiential learning. They chose the kitchen as the setting, since much of a family's interaction occurs in the kitchen during meal preparation, mealtime, and cleanup, and the kitchen, with all its gadgets, is an environment in which exploration and early social development can take place.

The Kitchen Curriculum, titled *Hey! What's Cooking?* presents suggestions for parents and can be used by educators to promote social interaction while teaching basic independent living skills. It begins with general guidelines for introducing the child to touch, taste, sound, and smell. It then presents tips for helping the child develop skills in performing daily tasks, survival cooking, and cleanup, so the child becomes a contributing member of the family unit. The ultimate goal is to ensure that the child has the opportunity to develop a sense of independence and self-worth.

Although the kitchen environment may pose some initial danger, protecting the child from such experiences can be just as dangerous. A child who is deprived of experience does not continue to seek new experiences; he or she may become less curious and less motivated to learn new concepts and ideas.

The skills and suggestions provided in the Kitchen Curriculum are arranged according to chronological age of the child, but the authors recognize that the development of each visually impaired child is different and that the activities outlined for each age range are merely guidelines. Although most of the activities presented in the curriculum are designed specifically for preschool- and elementary-aged children, they could be used with older children.

Strategies

Each activity is designed to develop a close working relationship between the parent or caregiver and the child. Through the acquisition of such skills, the child begins to gain a sense of self-worth and social competence. Many of the activities focus on the importance of appropriate social behavior or the acquisition of a specific social skill, such as eye contact. For example, the activities for 2-3-year-olds (see Table 1 in the appendix at the end of this chapter) encourage independence and a sense of responsibility while promoting interactive communication skills.

In performing specific household chores, the child develops a sense of self-sufficiency, learns how to ask for help in initiating or completing a task, and expands his or her expressive language. The parents or caretakers can encourage discussions of the shape, form, texture, and size of items used for particular chores by asking open-ended questions, such as, "Tell me all about this napkin" or "Tell me some ways you can use the napkin." While talking with the child or prompting statements, they can give positive cues to the appropriate direction of gaze or body posture. Such information helps the child to recognize what is expected of him or her within appropriate social contexts. Several illustrations of activities are presented in Table 1. (The entire Kitchen Curriculum is available from Franczeska Naughton, South Metropolitan Association for Low Incidence Handicapped Children, 800 Governors Highway, Flossmore, IL 60422.)

PEER-MEDIATED SOCIAL-SKILLS TRAINING

Although the peer-mediated intervention described in Chapter 6 used only elementary-school-aged visually impaired students, similar procedures could be initiated with other age groups, particularly adolescents. The training strategies were most effective when performed in a resource room or in a special day-class environment. The structure and consistency of such settings provide visually impaired and sighted students with a variety of alternatives for play and relaxed interactions.

When social-skills training occurs in natural contexts with competent visually impaired or sighted age-mates, it has far-reaching effects on the generalization and maintenance of appropriate social behaviors. Generalization can occur when certain strategies are used.

Strategies

1. Develop role-play scenarios that are representative of the student's experiences in school, at home, and in the community.

2. Use sighted or visually impaired age-mates who have a core of friends and who are interested in interacting with the visually impaired student.

3. Provide opportunities for peers to give feedback to the visually impaired student, monitored by the teacher of visually impaired students or the social-skills trainer in a constructive manner.

4. Develop social-skills training activities that take place in natural environments.

5. Provide environments and situations in which the visually impaired student can learn to play and understand the rules of an array of games and activities.

6. To ensure consistency, communicate closely with parents or caregivers, classroom teachers, or employers regarding the student's social competence.

7. To promote the acquisition and maintenance of targeted social behaviors, teach the student such self-monitoring strategies as the use of skills checklists, interactive videos, or verbal discussion.

BEHAVIORAL CONTRACTS

Along with a structured social-skills training procedure, visually impaired students (especially those who are preparing for an integrated classroom experience who have some difficulty working independently or interacting effectively in a group environment) can benefit from behavioral contracts that reinforce appropriate social behavior in a variety of educational and community settings. These contracts may incorporate self-monitoring techniques in which the reminder of a tangible cue (that is, written contracts on their desks) stimulates appropriate social behavior.

We have used behavioral contracts in special day classes at regular education sites and at a state school, where some of the students were in residence and others were day students. The contracts were modified to include mainstream experiences when the students needed help with them. The strategies that follow can be used to implement these contracts.

Strategies

1. Attach a written statement to the student's desk in either large print or braille, which includes:

a. A statement of the period involved (for example, by Friday afternoon or every day this week or from the beginning of the day until the first recess).

b. A statement of the goal to be achieved (for instance, "I will earn [set a number] of [note the markers given]") that will be attached to the contract, so the student can monitor his or her progress. Scratch-and-sniff stickers and brightly colored stickers are successful markers for young students, and file "flag" dots and holes made with a paper punch are successful for middle elementary and older students.

c. The behaviors to be achieved (such as, "raising my hand for help," "waiting my turn," "working at my desk").

d. The reward to be gained at the end of the period (for example, a certificate for free time to be "spent" on a favorite activity, the selection of something from the "prize box," and so forth).

2. Review the document with the student on a regular schedule, beginning with short periods and then extending the time over which the behaviors sought are noted. Be consistent with rewarding the behavior; attach a paper punch to your belt or carry dots in your pocket. A "runner's" watch is useful because you can set it to remind yourself that it is time to monitor a behavior or to remind students that an agreed-upon time limit is up.

3. Identify with students the specific behaviors that are expected. We met with each student once a week to review the general contract and to identify something special they were working on. These conferences gave us an opportunity to talk about why rocking, eye poking, or head turning was targeted. In addition, it gave us an idea of how the students were responding; in one case, we discovered that a particular student, who had a severe hearing impairment, knew the signs only for "angry" and "happy." We added new signs for emotions and responses and included their appropriate uses the goals stated in the contract.

4. For younger students, stickers themselves can be the goal, and they will want to take them at the end of each period of monitoring. When a period is extended, the teacher can add free-time tokens or certificates; time at favorite activities; and the "prize box," which contains tangible rewards that may increase the student's interest in grooming, recreation, or personal orga-

nization and that you can teach him or her to use. Prizes may include samples of perfume, after-shave, hand lotion, makeup, toothpaste, or deodorant; combs, toothbrushes, key rings, wallets, inexpensive book bags or totes, inexpensive athletic totes, lip glosses or chapsticks, heavy paper folders, signature guides, small binders for braille notes, braille erasers, and inexpensive cassette tapes.

5. The teacher can extend the contract to include such prizes as permission to travel to another classroom or school, to travel independently, to collect and deliver homework, and to participate in extra-curricular activities. The contract may be dropped when the student achieves full participation in the mainstream environment, socially as well as academically. (Examples of behavioral contracts can be obtained from the first author.)

PHYSICAL SKILLS

Many social interactions are learned visually through imitation and modeling. Appropriate social behaviors that are taken for granted are learned incidentally at a very young age and are not consciously thought of when one engages in social interactions. For example, persons who are sighted know that there is a field of "personal space" that is viewed differently in different cultures, that people face one another while conversing, and that posture or gestures can be statements or affect the impact of statements. Visually impaired children, however, require direct intervention to learn these common assumptions about the utilization of appropriate physical behavior.

The development of such physical skills is critical to the interactive ability of visually impaired students and can be incorporated into a variety of program models. Training of such physical skills can easily be infused into group discussions in special day classes or resource rooms or taught to individual itinerant students as part of the work of increasing or decreasing a targeted social behavior. The strategies outlined here can be used with a wide range of severely visually impaired students, as well as those with multiple disabilities.

Strategies

Several specific examples of physical behaviors that require training are presented for individual and group instruction. When developing intervention strategies for visually impaired students in a mainstream, vocational, or community-based program, the teacher needs to follow some general guidelines, which are listed below:

1. The student should be prepared for the intervention. Many children and adolescents are concerned about their appearance and behavior, but they are defensive about direct approaches to change them. Therefore, an approach that stresses from the outset the rewards of changed appearance or behavior has distinct advantages.

2. Target the items on which you and the student will work. Identify the strategies you will use and preface the need for changes by providing information on what posture, body movement, gesture, and body position communicate to persons who are sighted.

3. Use positive reinforcement strategies, and ensure that others involved (parents, support staff, siblings) use the same positive approach.

For students with a multiplicity of challenges, behavior management strategies are useful. Target the behavior sought and ensure that adequate baseline data are obtained. Use reinforcement techniques that are known to be successful with the student.

Eye Contact

It is difficult to convey the import of this skill when performing it is virtually impossible for the child who has no vision, has a cosmetic problem, or has vision that is so limited that the concept of "gaze" is meaningless. Thus, it is helpful to use the following alternative descriptions of what is needed:

1. "People face each other when speaking."
2. "If you face me, I know that you're paying attention."
3. "When your face is pointed to the floor [or the desk top, or your ear is turned to me], I don't know whether you are talking with me or someone else."

For the child who has multiple disabilities, visual or auditory stimulation or both can accomplish the same goal. The following are two examples:

1. Use a bright toy (such as a pinwheel, a battery-operated toy, or

a tape recorder) and pair it with the child's gaze. Reinforce the head turn and keep the object close to the face. Fade the toy and continue to reinforce head turns toward the face of the speaker.

2. Pair a handshake with a light touch to the face, turning the child's face to the speaker. Reinforce the light touch with a statement or an extra handshake.

Gestures

All students can be taught gestures in one setting or another. For one child, simply learning to extend a hand as a gesture of good-bye and hello is a significant increase in communication. For another child, learning to wave a car past, to shake hands, to "flag" a waitress, or to raise a hand to an oncoming bus means independence and improved communication. The following strategies may be useful in teaching these gestures:

1. Determine the level of gesture communication that is appropriate to the student. Use community-based activities when possible, because the reinforcement comes more quickly from peers and the public than from only staff members and family members.

2. Most severely visually impaired students will need some motor prompting or motor support to learn gestures. When appropriate, give a verbal cue along with motor support.

3. For the student who signs, you should carefully observe the gestures that are used. Manual communication may occur only within the field of the student's vision, and much information about other gestures may be missing.

4. Rehearse gestures either by consistent sequences of motor-support intervention or through instruction and practice.

5. Prompt or support the student in using the gestures in such places as the playground and at the bus stop.

6. Encourage independent expression by gesture through the wider use of gestures in the environment.

Body Language

It is important for the student to master some skills relating to posture, gaze, turns, and gestures before dealing with body language. Therefore, the skills discussed here should be taught to students who have mastered some physical-communication skills. Social-skills groups are useful for these activities.

1. Using motor support, help the student to make a fist and then to shake it. Discuss the possible messages inherent in shaking a fist at another person. Have the student lean forward and come very close to another student, speaking loudly. Discuss the physical messages here.

2. Describe some of the basic body-language messages (any work on the subject will provide the information) and then assist the student to demonstrate them. Relaxation exercises (deep breathing, head rolls, and shoulder lifts) are useful in preparing students for movement. After these exercises, the student can practice hunched shoulders and clenched fists, followed by a dropped head and loose arms and then erect posture and comfortable arm and leg stances.

3. Use role playing for the student and his or her peers and for the student and the staff as practice.

4. Introduce the concept of the "double message"—an assertive request with an aggressive stance and an aggressive statement with a passive stance. Students with limited vision and a hearing impairment have found these activities useful in improving their communication skills in general.

5. Have the student demonstrate his or her body-language skills to family members, peers, and the staff (particularly the orientation and mobility staff), and support the student's use of appropriate body language in community activities.

Inappropriate Movement

Inappropriate movements, such as rocking, eye poking, and head rolling, are a major concern of all sighted people who have frequent contact with the visually impaired child. The following strategies may be useful in this regard:

1. Determine where the behaviors occur and ensure, through consultation with a physical or occupational therapist, that the behavior can and should be addressed by family and staff without the assistance of the therapist.

2. Use behavior modification techniques to determine the baseline level of movements, goals, and intervention strategies.

3. Some students will respond to a stimulus that reminds them that they are moving (one student wore a small bell in the rubber band that held her pony tail; she preferred to correct herself without reinforcement from another person).

4. Other students prefer to choose a setting in which they work on diminishing a behavior while remaining free to demonstrate it elsewhere. This preference may be used to introduce the idea of privacy and private places, helping the student to distinguish rocking on a bus, for example, from rocking while relaxing in the privacy of one's room.

5. It is difficult to teach appropriate facial expressions. However, try to help students to reduce such inappropriate expressions as smiling while relating sad news, and include some general information while working on body language.

Table 2 at the end of this chapter presents some specific curricular strategies for training physical behaviors in a structured group format. Attainment of each targeted physical behavior is written in terms of a behavioral goal and objective. Then specific methods and evaluation procedures are presented to help the child acquire the target skill.

ASSERTIVENESS TRAINING

Once visually impaired students have developed a set of socially competent behaviors, they should apply them in assertive interactions with peers, adults, co-workers, and potential employers. One concern expressed by professionals who work with visually impaired students is that the students' behavior seems passive or aggressive, rather than assertive (Rickelman & Blaylock, 1983); for example, that students use a hostile tone of voice, make negative statements, and fail to maintain eye contact and to use appropriate body posture were apparent in contacts with others (Van Hasselt, Hersen, & Kazdin, 1984).

In their work with visually impaired students in a classroom, Harrel and Strauss (1986) have successfully used journal writing, sentence-completion exercises, role playing, and self-help groups to promote assertive behavior. They have also found that interaction with other, competent visually impaired individuals fosters assertive behavior and the chance to share experiences that are unique to visually impaired persons.

Assertiveness training seems to be most effective in a group format where the students have similar cognitive or functional abilities. Self-monitoring, with feedback from video and audiotapes, is useful in developing assertive behavior.

Because assertive behavior involves higher-order skills and techniques, it should be taught to secondary-level students with good oral or signing communication skills. It is also helpful for nondisabled peers to participate in the assertiveness training sessions to demonstrate appropriate behavior and to provide feedback. The following activities described incorporate the utilization of assertive behavior in real-life experiences, so the students can apply the skills learned during training to travel experiences, shopping encounters, dating experiences, and interactions with co-workers or supervisors.

Strategies

1. Demonstrate passive, assertive, and aggressive responses. (For example, complete the sentence, "If I want help at the store, I could _____.")

2. Have the students demonstrate responses in given situations. (For example, tell the students "If you want to obtain information on the telephone or get assistance at a bus stop or directions on the street, show me a passive [aggressive or assertive way] of asking.")

3. Identify with the students which responses they like to receive.

4. Video-tape or tape-record the sessions and play them back to the students.

5. Identify with the students the connotations of the styles they have demonstrated: aggression = anger, a threat, and rudeness; passivity = fear and an "I don't matter" attitude; assertion = confidence, ability, and independence.

6. Associate posture, gestures, and personal space with communication (see the "Physical Skills" section for further discussion): aggression = fist shaking and foot stomping; passivity = head down and the exhibition of mannerisms with silence; and assertion = erect posture and gaze directed at others.

7. Record sessions emphasizing the tone of voice: aggression = shouting or a demanding tone; passivity = silence, whispering, and long pauses before requests or statements; assertion = an

audible voice, clear statements or requests, and the use of courteous language.

8. Practice behaviors in actual settings. Each student should do the following:
   a. Make a telephone call to a store or business for information.
   b. Request information or assistance on public transportation.
   c. Request assistance or directions while shopping.
   d. Identify the person or place in a grocery store where assistance can be obtained (for example, the checkout stand, or the manager's station).

9. The student should develop a repertoire of opening statements, such as these:
   a. "I would like assistance with my shopping today. Please let me know when a clerk is available."
   b. "Please let me know when we reach Main Street—I need to make my transfer there."

10. For students who use alternative communication skills:
    a. Deaf-blind students who use teletouch and can speak should include a clearly visible statement on the cover, for example: "Hello. This is a teletouch, which I need to communicate with you. Please use it as you would use a regular typewriter." The student should learn to take the teletouch to a counter or checkout (which requires orientation to the shopping area), place the teletouch on the counter, and say, "May I have assistance when someone is available?"
    b. For nonspeaking deaf-blind students, learning to present a list (made independently or with assistance) is similar, except that the list is presented without a statement.
    c. For students with low vision who have some typing ability and who are hearing or verbally impaired, a hand-held communicator that prints what is typed in is useful.

11. Identify situations in which passive or aggressive behaviors are both useful and appropriate:
    a. When touched by a stranger on public transportation, a loud request to be left alone may be necessary.
    b. For visually impaired persons who cannot tell the source or cause of a disturbance while traveling, simply moving closer to a checkout, a taxi stand, the bus driver, the office

location in a store, and the like to request help is preferable to trying to ascertain what is happening.

c. Have the students add to this list and discuss responses that will ensure assistance.

12. Have the students carry tape recorders with them into the community and help them review the interactions they have experienced. Rehearse possible variations of encounters before they go out again and use a series of tapes to help the students evaluate their own success.

Table 3 at the end of this chapter presents activities through which the instructor can promote and facilitate assertive behavior for his or her students by helping them to identify emotions and expressions of emotions. Each activity relates to a specific goal and set of program objectives. Furthermore, each objective includes guidelines and suggestions for successful implementation.

CONCLUSION

The activities and strategies presented in this chapter provide a foundation for the development of social competence by visually impaired students in integrated school and community environments. However, the suggested interventions are only a framework for further investigation and implementation. To incorporate social-skills interventions into a traditional educational context, practitioners must gain the cooperation and support of program administrators, parents, and students and be creative, flexible, and committed to initiating and implementing such practices. If we educators of visually impaired students intend to provide services that prepare students for future life endeavors, then we must be willing to develop skills and to create service-delivery models that allow teachers to integrate a more functionally based curriculum.

The acquisition of social skills is not a natural occurrence for visually impaired children; these skills require training and must be nurtured throughout students educational years. The intervention strategies set forth in this chapter, as well as those that have been described in other chapters, have enhanced the abilities of students not only to interact effectively with sighted peers and adults, but to make independent decisions, to take responsibility for their actions, and to feel confident and successful within the sighted environment.

CHAPTER 8, APPENDIX

Table 1. Kitchen Curriculum Activities

CHILDREN AGED 2–3

1 Allow the child to experience the function of movable parts by spraying plants, squirting detergent in a bowl, opening cans, and helping to scoop ice cream.
2. Begin household chores.
   a. Have the child carry napkins to the table.
   b. If samples of food are available, such as carrot sticks, say "Bring the carrot stick to Daddy [or some other family member]."
   c. Place frequently used utensils where the child can reach them, and ask the child to give you the pan, the measuring cup, the serving spoon, and similar items.
3. Increase the child's exposure to different textures and tastes, such as the softness of flour, the grittiness of sugar, the moistness of butter, the sliminess of eggs, and the feel of dough. Include the child in one or more steps of cooking and baking. Let the child feel the raw dough and mold it like clay and then experience the taste and temperature of newly baked products.

CHILDREN AGED 3–4

1. Have the child help with household chores:
   a. Folding napkins.
   b. Bringing utensils to the table.
   c. Returning dishes to the table.
   d. Pushing food scraps off plates into the wastebasket. This is good early training for search-exploring techniques that are essential to a wide range of activities.
2. Have the child assist in cooking.
   a. Stirring batter.
   b. Shredding lettuce and preparing salads and vegetables.
   c. Mixing powder with liquid, such as chocolate milk and pudding. The child will need to check his or her progress in mixing by using his or her fingers. Fingers are efficient tools, and a blind child must learn to substitute touch for sight. The wise parent quickly accepts what may appear to be messy and unsavory as an essential step in learning. From 3 to 4 years, the child is also gaining independence in washing his or her hands. Helping in the kitchen provides many opportunities to clean hands, too.
3. Use cooking and baking activities to help the child become aware of time. Adapt a kitchen timer for visual impairment by raising dots or enlarging the minute signs with nail polish or glue, and use it to alert the child to the time it takes to:
   a. Bake cookies.
   b Cool pudding.
   c. Freeze ice cubes.

CHILDREN AGED 4–5

1. Let the child assist in more household chores by:
   a. Learning the correct table placement and helping to set the table.
   b. Putting cheese on crackers and meat on bread.

(continued on next page)

Table 1. *continued*

    c. Spooning jelly on bread. (This will probably be a messy task, but it will pre-pare the child for later tasks and is a tasty job.)

2. Teach the child to use left- and right-side orientation skills. Teach the child that the knife is placed on the right side of the plate, the fork on the left side, the cup in front of the knife, and the chair behind the plate.

3. Table manners. Set standards of appropriate behavior at the table. Because of the importance of practice, the family of the visually impaired child will benefit if meals are regularly scheduled and eaten together and high standards of behavior are maintained. Learning good manners is important for later social-ization away from home. Socially acceptable eating habits and manners are the right of every visually impaired child. They do not come naturally, however; they have to be learned.

    a. Use "please" and "thank-you" regularly.

    b. Pass food around the table; do not always serve the child. Teach the child such table manners as taking one roll and not feeling every roll.

    c. Wait for the child to ask for a helping; do not anticipate his or her every need.

4. Introduce the fork. Use of the spoon is now well established. In teaching the child how to use a fork, identify and maintain the appropriate use. For exam-ple, insist that the fork be used for meat and pancakes. Do not let the child revert to using his or her fingers. The child may use a stabbing motion until he or she the child is comfortable with the fork. With greater practice, the child should be encouraged to use a slower, smoother, rhythmic movement. At this age, the child will use one hand to locate bite-size pieces of food and the other to pierce them.

CHILDREN AGED 5–6

1. Let the child help with still more household chores.

    a. Increase the child's independence in completing previous tasks.

    b. Allow the child to fill glasses with assistance. (During the child's early years, buy quart containers or transfer liquids from larger containers to a pitcher.)

    c. Teach the child to spread butter, peanut butter, and jelly.

2. Table Manners.

    a. Let the child serve his or her own food at the table and practice putting the appropriate amount of food on a spoon.

    b. Discourage the use of the hands to eat and encourage the use of a spoon and fork. Do not rush the child. Make the dinner hour a pleasant family sharing time and allow plenty of time (an extra 15 minutes at least) for the child to carry out good manners.

3. Supplement cooking tasks by discussing the different textures of foods as con-ditions change. For example, cookies change from soft to hard during the bak-ing–cooling process. Review touching, molding, smelling, and tasting with more emphasis on change.

Table 2. Physical Skills: Strategies for Training in a Structured Group Format

Goals: *The students will be able to define body language and describe it as communication and will demonstrate the ability to show a change in posture, use a gesture, and display a functional knowledge of body language.*

Curricular Item	Instruction to the Teacher	Students' Behavior and Evaluation	Assessment Criterion
The students will define body language as communication.	1. Discuss the concept of body language. 2. Discuss the various things communicated by posture gesture, and personal space. 3. Add body language to the list of items describing communication.	The class will define body language as a communication device. The class will be able to name at least one item expressed through body language.	90 percent class accuracy 90 percent class accuracy
The students will develop a repertoire of behaviors that demonstrate the use of body language.	1. Have the students discuss and practice in class various body communications, such as touching and leaning forward or back. 2. Have the students demonstrate various body-language messages on cue.	The class will demonstrate the ability to display a rehearsed body communication on cue from the teacher.	80 percent class accuracy

(continued on next page)

Table 2. continued

Curricular Item	Instruction to the Teacher	Students' Behavior and Evaluation	Assessment Criterion
Goals: *The students will define a mannerism as an inappropriate form of body language or behavior and will reduce the display of a selected mannerism on cue.*			
The students will identify various behaviors as "mannerisms."	1. In a class discussion, ask the students to name rocking, eye poking, hand waving, and so forth, as mannerisms.	Individual students or the class will be able to identify at least two behaviors as mannerisms.	90 percent individual or class accuracy
The students will be able to cite reasons for discontinuing the mannerisms.	1. In a class discussion, ask the students to name the negative consequences of mannerisms (poor response from strangers and friends, cosmetic changes, for example).	The class will be able to identify at three negative results least of mannerisms.	90 percent class accuracy
The students will identify settings in which the expressions of mannerisms is acceptable.	1. Review the definitions of public and private. 2. Identify private areas where students may choose to express mannerisms.	The class will be able to identify that such behaviors may be performed in private and to name at least two appropriate private places where the expression of mannerisms is acceptable.	90 percent class accuracy
The student or students will respond to an agreed contract to reduce mannerisms.	1. Identify behaviors you wish to alter. 2. Identify the cue statement or activity. 3. Practice responses to the cue. 4. Establish rewards for the class's responses to the cue.	The class will respond to an established cue by diminishing the identified behavior.	90 percent class accuracy

Table 3. Assertiveness Skills: Strategies for Training in a Structured Group Format

Goals: *The students will identify feelings by name, recognize self-expressions of emotions, and recognize expressions of similar emotions by others.*

Curricular Item	Instruction to the Teacher	Students' Behavior and Evaluation	Assessment Criterion
The class will identify love, hate, anger, joy, jealousy, and happiness as emotions or feelings.	1. Name various emotions and feelings in a class discussion. 2. Describe the causes of the named emotions—events that precipitate emotional responses.	1. The students will name at least three feelings when the teacher asks them to do so. 2. The students will describe a feeling and the event that caused it.	90 percent class accuracy
The class will describe their own expressions of emotions or feelings.	1. Name typical expressions of emotions (such as shouting in anger, and laughing when happy). 2. Name individual responses and behaviors.	The students will be able to describe at least one sign of an emotion or feeling they have experienced.	90 percent class accuracy
The class will describe signs of emotion and feelings in others.	1. Have the class review expressions of various emotions. 2. Have the class name possible feelings others have when they are crying, laughing, shouting, and so on.	The students will be able to describe one possible feeling from a description of the behavior of another.	90 percent class accuracy
The class will discuss the fact that all people have similar emotions and feelings.	1. Lead a class discussion about the fact that all people have feelings. 2. Lead a class discussion about possible emotional responses to specific situations.	The students will agree with the teacher's statement that all people have feelings. The students will be able to give two examples of responses to a situation, such as anger shown through crying or shouting, as different expressions of the same emotion.	90 percent class accuracy
			75 percent class accuracy

(continued on next page)

Table 3. *continued*

Curricular Item	Instruction to the Teacher	Students' Behavior and Evaluation	Assessment Criterion
Goals: *The students will define communication as the sharing of ideas, feelings, needs, and information and will define modes of communication.*			
The students will define communication as the sharing of ideas and feelings.	1. Review the feelings previously discussed. 2. Share an idea. 3. Define the telling of feelings or ideas to others as communication.	1. The students will identify the sharing of an idea or a feelingas communication.	90 percent class accuracy
The students will define communication as the sharing of needs and information.	1. Have the students discuss the meanings of "need" and "information." 2. Help the students define the sharing of needs and information as communication.	The students will define the words *need* and *information*, and identify sharing them as a form of communication.	90 percent class accuracy
The students will give reasons for communication and examples of the positive effects of communication skills.	1. In a class discussion, have the students identify reasons for sharing ideas, feelings, needs, and information 2. In a class discussion, have the students identify the value of communicating ideas, needs, feelings, and information.	1. The class will name at least three reasons for communication. 2. The class will be able to identify at least three positive effects of communication.	90 percent class accuracy
The students will define methods of communication other than speaking.	1. Have the class create a list of alternative modes of communication: tears, laughter, signing, hitting, throwing objects, holding hands, hugging, and the like.	The class will be able to name at least three examples of nonverbal communication.	90 percent class accuracy

Chapter 9
The Creative Games Project

Janet Macks

After I participated in a peer-directed social-skills training project (Sacks, 1987), I developed and carried out the Creative Games Project at an elementary school in San Francisco. At first, I worked with one visually impaired student and his nondisabled peers. However, my objective was not only to develop and teach specific social skills but to see if any newly acquired or learned social skills would be applied to the project's participating members as well as other visually impaired students at this school.

The Creative Games Project was based on playing cooperative, noncompetitive games. If they are played in a safe, supportive, and nonthreatening environment, games can help develop, teach, and provide training in specific social skills. Although the children played games to have fun, this experience gave me the opportunity to teach them skills relating to communication and helping, cooperation, positive interactions and initiations, and reactions to and relationships with people who are different.

Throughout the project, emphasis was placed on clarifying and, in some instances, eliminating established and existing attitudes toward blind and visually impaired individuals. First, however, the participating members were encouraged to take note of their similarities and differences so they could appreciate each person's abilities. Through cooperative and noncompetitive play, each student would soon realize that he or she could be both helped and helper, student and teacher.

BACKGROUND

In March 1987, a 10-year-old boy named Bob came to San Francisco from Taiwan. When he arrived, he spoke his native language, Mandarin Chinese, and only a few words of English. In Taiwan, Bob was seriously burned when a deranged man entered his classroom and poured sulfuric acid on the children. The acid caused total blindness in Bob's left eye, blurry vision in his right eye, and third-degree burns on his body and face. Although he has had plastic surgery, his face is severely disfigured.

The teacher of visually impaired children and the orientation and mobility instructor decided to hold a series of in-service training sessions for the teachers and students at the school to deal with their anticipated reactions, such as fear, anger, sadness, and shock, not only to Bob's blindness, but to his disfigurement. The initial sessions concentrated on the event that caused Bob's blindness and disfigurement, and later sessions focused on his positive attributes and abilities and on the similarities between Bob and the other children. As the principal said, "This is an opportunity for our students to learn to accept people who are different and not to judge people only by their appearance."

As a result of the in-service training, a club was formed, the Guardian Angels Club. The club consisted of a cross section of children—culturally, academically, and socially—in grades 1 to 6. It is interesting that many of the club members were "hard-to-handle children," many of whom were disruptive, inattentive, uncooperative, unmotivated, and had low self-esteem.

The Guardian Angels felt a great sense of pride and responsibility. Whether as peer tutors, English tutors, or members of the Creative Games Project, they took their new roles seriously. In their first meeting, they established the following pledge:

> As a member of the Guardian Angels, I pledge to stand up for Bob and to help others realize that he is a neat person inside. I pledge to help others look past appearances and judge people by the inside. To fulfill my obligation as a leader, I pledge to show others in a nice way how to treat him and others who are disabled.

Their commitment to their roles is evident in their statements of why they wanted to be Guardian Angels, such as the following:

> I would like to be Bob's guardian angel because I would like to make him feel at home here. I would be able to handle the responsibility and get over the way he looks. I would like to be

his friend. I will treat him as though he is not disfigured. I want him to feel comfortable at my school.

I can help Bob by being his friend and I could be a sighted guide for him. When I am a sighted guide for him, I could bring him around the school or the schoolyard. If I was his friend, I could teach him the English language or help him with his braille. If Bob got a letter that was not in braille, I could ask him if I should read it to him. If Bob needed more friends, then I could ask some of my friends to meet him. If anybody was laughing or teasing Bob, I would ask that person to be considerate. If that person wouldn't be considerate, then that person would be a maniac. If Bob needs anything, I always want to help.

THE PROJECT

After attending and participating in the initial Guardian Angel meetings, 10 students were selected to take part in the Creative Games Project. They were representative of the larger group in that they also were a cross section of the school's students—culturally, academically, chronologically, and socially.

For 10 weeks (once a week for 45 to 60 minutes), I worked with the 10 Guardian Angels and Bob. The children played games that could be played by children of various ages and abilities. To place all students on an equal footing, I taught games that were new to them. Many of these games came from the *New Games Book* (Flyegelman, 1976), an activity book that includes games in which the players are the most important contributors. Examples of the games initiated during the project follow.

"Rattlers," or the Predator-Prey Game

For this game, everyone forms a circle around two players, who are blindfolded. One of the two acts as the predator, and the other acts as the prey. Each one holds a can that has been filled with beans, pebbles, or similar items that make sounds (they can either sound the same or be filled with different objects so as to distinguish the predator from the prey). The outside circle of players are told that their job is to define the boundaries for the two blindfolded players. That is, they must make sure that neither the predator nor the prey wanders outside the circle. The game begins when the predator shakes his or her can. The prey must respond by shaking his or her can. The predator tries to catch the prey, and the prey tries to avoid being caught. The shaking of the cans continues until the predator catches the prey.

This game places the two players on an equal footing, for they are both playing as "blind" players and must use and pay attention to their other senses. It also presents the opportunity to teach all the participants about predator-prey relationships and food chains.

"The Blob"

This game requires total cooperation by the players. Initially, the children are paired up—a sighted child with a visually impaired child, or a sighted child with another sighted child who was blind-folded to simulate visual impairment—to avoid confusion during the game. The boundaries are set and are shown to the players. One player or, in this case, one group of players, is declared "it." When those who are "it" tag a child, that child or group must attach themselves to the original "it" by holding onto each others' hands. Thus, the blob grows. Now, instead of one or two being "it," anywhere from two to four are "it." The blob continues to grow with each addition. As a group, we decided that the blob could split itself, but that each blob had to contain a minimum of three players.

The game can become wild and confusing. Trying to keep track of the blobs, trying not to get whipped around when a blob gets too big, and trying to keep track of the boundaries are just some of the challenges. Although the pairs work together, the blobs provide opportunities for all who are part of the blob to develop teamwork, cooperation, and communication-listening skills (Are they going too fast or too slow? In what direction are you going?).

Since the sighted child must learn to describe to the visually impaired child the necessary information, he or she learns what information is needed and what is extraneous. The children also learn to pay attention to one another's needs and abilities and to trust each other. The visually impaired child must trust his or her partner, and the partner, in turn, must learn how to foster that trust and to communicate his or her trust. Finally, all the children experience what it is like to run around freely.

"Ooh-Ahh," or Pass the Squeeze

The children stand in a circle, all holding hands, and the teacher chooses one child to squeeze the hand of the player to his or her right. From then on, the squeeze is passed around the circle. The object of the game is to get the squeeze to travel as quickly as possible. The game can be adapted by (1) changing the direction in which the squeeze travels, (2) initiating simultaneous squeezes going in both directions, and (3) changing the game to the Ooh-Ahh game. In the Ooh-Ahh game, the right hand is Ooh and the left hand is Ahh. Depending on which way the squeeze is passed, the children will shout Ooh or Ahh as they squeeze the next player's hand.

Although this game is more passive than the others, it can become confusing when the players have to shout Ooh and Ahh. It is a good game for working on listening skills, cooperation, the use of right and left, following directions, and for breaking down barriers that come with holding hands with members of the opposite sex.

Parachute Games

A great deal can be done with just one parachute. In fact, many ideas came from the students themselves. The parachute was used in the following ways:

1. By holding its edges, the children lifted the parachute up and down and saw how high they could make it go, how quickly they could bring it to the ground, and how large a bubble they could make with the captured air.

2. The children ran around in a circle while holding onto the edges of the parachute.

3. Each child was assigned a number, and I called out numbers at random, either singly or in groups. When a student heard his or her number called, he or she tried to run under the parachute, while the others continued to raise and lower it as quickly as they could. The games played with the parachute offered the players the chance to create their own games and the rules to accompany the games.

"The Lap Sit"

For this game, participating players stand in a circle, shoulder to shoulder. They are instructed to turn to their right and take one step into the center of the circle. Counting to three, they all gently sit down on the lap of the person behind them. It is hoped that they will all sit down at the same time and form a circle. If they do so and all are "comfortably" seated, then they can give back or shoulder rubs to the person in front of them. The game can be changed so the players take more than one step and alternate their feet or lift their right feet and arms and then lift their left feet and arms as they walk into the center.

In the end, the Lap Sit was more fun than it was successful. Although attempts to make a sitting circle were unsuccessful, everyone worked together as a team and, from the shouts of laughter, all the children had fun.

TRAINING

As is true of all projects, it is important that members have a clear understanding of the project's goals and objectives. Therefore, during the first session with the Guardian Angels, I led a discussion of the objectives of playing the games with Bob. Although the group talked at great length, one objective was not verbalized: to give Bob the opportunity to experience the joys and challenges of playing with a group of peers.

The discussion began with one unanimous objective: Every member of the group agreed that they would do anything to "help Bob." Therefore, we talked about what was necessary to achieve this objective. First, we talked about the importance of always working cooperatively as a group. Then, we discussed the need to take into account the facts that Bob did not speak English and was visually impaired. The Guardian Angels said they would try to explain things to Bob as simply as they could and, when possible, to apply their limited Mandarin Chinese. They also briefly mentioned his visual impairment, but agreed that "it didn't matter." We went on to discuss the importance of each team member and emphasized that he or she had something unique to offer and that each person on the team had his or her own needs. In time, they all realized that they would not only need to be helped but would be the helpers and that for the group to work, they would have to pay attention to each person's needs. Although the project was formed for Bob, I wanted each participant to come away with skills that could be applied to any situation.

The first game session was spent playing the Predator-Prey game. Although it took a fair amount of time to explain the game to the group and then to Bob, we did manage to play a few rounds of the game before the time was up. The Guardian Angels did their best to show Bob how to play, but they were very confused because they had never before been in such a situation. Before the time was up, I spent a few minutes discussing what we had just done. I reassured the players that each person would get his or her turn at this game and then asked the group "Why did we play this particular game?" The response was, once again, unanimous: "We are playing to help Bob, to teach him these games."

The following week, we played the Predator-Prey game a second time. First, I reviewed the rules of the game, and then the Guardian Angels refreshed Bob's memory and we carried on with the game. Two of the youngest Guardian Angels did not want to play because they were afraid of being blindfolded. At first, the older players put a great deal of pressure on them to play, but after a short discussion about the need to support and trust one another, we resumed the game without them. The other players did their best to alleviate the fears of the frightened young players. Before the game time was up, these two youngest members of the group willingly participated in the game and came away from the experience with smiles on their faces. Again, I led a short discussion by asking two questions: "Why do you think we played this game?" and "What did you learn from playing this game?" The group briefly talked about what it felt like to be temporarily blind and the importance of paying attention to one's other senses, such as hearing.

Although I had a specific agenda for each play session, the group's plans would often change. The number of participating Guardian Angels would fluctuate each week, as would the students' energy level. Their moods would often determine the activity for a given day. Regardless of the games played, we would always hold a discussion at the end of our group time.

As our time together continued, this small group of 10 children became close. When problems arose, we would discuss them until all members felt a sense of resolution. While they supported each other, they developed a great sense of respect for one another. Furthermore, about halfway through the project, we decided to include five other visually impaired students. The Guardian Angels exhibited the same sensitivity to the new members as they did to Bob and their other peers. Each person learned from the next, and although the children's sensitivity was not often verbalized, it was evident by their patience, interest, and willingness to be flexible, helpful, and supportive.

At the end of the project, the staff gave the Guardian Angels a party. I asked each member what he or she would remember most and take with him or her from being a Guardian Angel. The following are some of the responses:

"We can teach them, and we might learn something
ourselves."
"I like working with the visually impaired kids; they've taught
me things."
"It made me feel good."
"I liked helping."
"I liked playing the games and I liked teaching Bob the
games."
"I care about him."
"I liked playing the games. They can do everything, even
some things I can't do."

DISCUSSION

The social-skills training that took place during the Creative
Games Project seemed to have a greater effect on the Guardian
Angels than on the visually impaired students. As was previously
mentioned, the 10 students who were chosen for this project were
what many considered to be disruptive and hard to handle. Within
the short period I spent with them, I not only saw personalities
change but heard from both their parents and the teachers that
they, too, saw positive changes in them. The children became less
disruptive in their classrooms and offered to help their teachers
and fellow students. While these students became more assertive,
they also developed a greater sensitivity to those around them.
Each member of the Creative Games Project was given a great
deal of responsibility. The result was increased self-esteem and
more positive self-images.

Bob and other visually impaired students also benefited from
this project. Bob was immediately accepted by a friendly and supportive group of peers, given the chance to learn English, and
included in all aspects of life in the school. Whether in the classroom, the cafeteria, the playground, or the project, he learned to
work as a cooperating and trusting member of a team of peers.
The other visually impaired students were given the chance to
take part in the special project that was originally designed to
"help Bob." By further teaching the Guardian Angels about necessary communication with and helping skills for visually impaired
individuals, they were able to be both participants and teachers.

Despite the differences in age, sex, and social, cultural, and
academic standing, the group members learned to concentrate on
each person's abilities and individual needs. In realizing the similarities of all people, they learned to care and trust those who, for
one reason or another, appear to be "different." By playing the

cooperative and noncompetitive games and discussing the positive and negative aspects of our game time, the members realized they could be both teachers and students and that they could be both helped and helpers. They learned how to improve their communication skills to learn a person's needs, rather than assuming and making judgments about what a person's needs might be. They also learned the appropriate use of assertive or, in some cases, unassertive behavior.

The Guardian Angels looked forward to our games together—they wanted to help teach Bob. What they did not initially realize, however, was the carryover of learned skills and behaviors into other areas of their lives. In the end, they all came away from the project with skills and behaviors that could be applied to the many facets of their lives—with their families, their communities, and their classmates, both disabled and nondisabled.

Chapter 10

Approaches to Increasing Assertive Behavior and Communication Skills in Blind and Visually Impaired Persons

Rona L. Pogrund and Felice A. Strauss

It has been shown that many visually impaired individuals are more often passive than assertive in their interactions with others (Burlingham, 1965; Imamura, 1965; Petruci, 1953; Rickelman & Blaylock, 1983; Sandler, 1963; Warren, 1977; Wilson, 1967). Visually impaired people are often successful academically and/or in vocational skills, yet they lack effective communication skills that would enable them to assert themselves in interpersonal relationships. Rickelman and Blaylock (1983) noted the passivity with which many of the blind subjects in their study responded when they were treated in ways which they did not like. This study suggested the need for blind people to become actively involved in systematic assertiveness training sessions to practice positive ways of expressing their feelings. Visually impaired people need to know the impact of verbal and nonverbal messages and how their

Reprinted with permission from the *Journal of Visual Impairment & Blindness* (June 1986), published by the American Foundation for the Blind, where it originally appeared under the names of Rona L. Harrell and Felice A. Strauss. The references that originally appeared as part of this article are listed in "References" at the back of this book.

passivity or aggressiveness affects others. With such an under-standing, visually impaired individuals will have more options from which to choose as they interact with others.

Since many behaviors of passivity and learned helplessness are acquired at an early age, learning alternative behaviors should begin early and continue to be reinforced as the visually impaired person matures. Thus, intervention techniques should be offered in the school curriculum and in the rehabilitation process to allevi-ate these problems. Such programs would offer positive ways to communicate more effectively with others.

LEARNED HELPLESSNESS AND THE CONCEPT OF CONTROL

The concept of control is extremely important psychologically; the more control an individual has over the environment, the greater the chance for success. Learned helplessness is a perception of the lack of control, whether or not that perception is accurate (Seligman, 1975). Family members, rehabilitation personnel, and teachers of the visually impaired can foster helplessness or increase its occurrence by creating an environment that is not close to reality. Continually reducing assignments for the visually impaired child, eliminating difficult tasks, or doing a task for the individual because it is easier for a sighted person to do so, are all symptoms of lowered expectations, often resulting in learned help-lessness.

If the blind or partially sighted individual has no experience in coping with anxiety and frustration or never fails and never over-comes failure, then that person will probably feel and act helpless when first confronted with failure. If one continually tries to make life fun and interesting for the visually impaired person and never gives the individual responsibilities, then the ability to tolerate boredom, failure, and frustration will not develop. Instead of creat-ing an unrealistic environment for such an individual, reasons should be given for both failure and success. For example, one can say, "You did not succeed because you did not try, not be-cause you have a visual impairment," or, "You succeeded because you are intelligent and have the ability."

The concept of competence mediates both failure and self-esteem. If an individual feels competent, then a temporary experi-ence of uncontrollability is attributed to external or unstable factors such as bad luck, lack of effort, or difficulty of a specific task. Conversely, if a person feels incompetent, then success will be attributed to external factors and failure to internal causes (Seligman, 1975).

Parents, teachers, and rehabilitation counselors of the visually impaired need to foster a feeling of competency by giving responsibilities to the visually impaired individual. These responsibilities at school can include such simple tasks as having students get booklists from teachers, handling peer problems (i.e., teasing or isolation), finishing uncompleted assignments for homework, circulating school bulletins, caring for plants or animals, or being responsible for a bulletin board or daily calendar. Rehabilitation personnel can have the visually impaired person identify possible places of employment, initiate contacts, call the bus company for transportation information, submit requests for equipment, etc. Parents should be urged to give their child chores to do regardless of how simple they are (i.e., setting a table, folding laundry, etc.), so that the individual can feel he or she is a contributing member of the family.

All people need to develop a strong self-concept and be responsible for their own actions. As for the visually impaired, too often sighted people are ready to do for them. It is important they learn to do for *themselves* so that they will not feel ineffective and become passive, allowing others to control their lives. If a visually impaired individual has already fallen into the passive role, it is important that he or she be encouraged to change these behaviors through concerted efforts in a highly structured program. Just as helplessness is learned, so can it be unlearned, and new, more assertive behaviors can replace passive actions.

FOUNDATIONS OF ASSERTIVENESS TRAINING

The basis for all assertiveness training is to be able to identify one's feelings and to verbalize them to others. Assertion training emphasizes both skill development and anxiety reduction. Being assertive means being able to verbally and nonverbally communicate one's positive and negative feelings and thoughts, without experiencing undue amounts of anxiety or guilt and without violating the dignity of others. Being assertive means taking responsibility for what happens to oneself in life. It enables one to make free choices for oneself without giving others the power to do so.

If one is assertive, one can protect oneself from being victimized and taken advantage of by others. Many visually impaired individuals fall into a "helpless" or "victim" role and need to learn ways to be freed from this position. For example, when at a restaurant or store it is not uncommon for the waitress or clerk to talk to the blind person's sighted companion, rather than to the blind person directly. The blind individual needs to communicate the desire to be treated as a competent equal, rather than as a nonperson.

Assertiveness rests upon a foundation of self-respect, respect for others, and respect for one's value system apart from others. Assertion training does not teach people "how to get their own way." The result of being assertive is, however, that one's needs are more often met.

ASSERTIVE, NONASSERTIVE, AND AGGRESSIVE BEHAVIORS

It is helpful to have a clear understanding at the outset of the differences between assertive, nonassertive, and aggressive behaviors. The nonassertive person is one who generally allows others to choose for him and, unfortunately, seldom achieves his desired goals. At the other extreme are those so aggressive that they usually get their way at the expense of others. Often, aggressiveness masks self-doubt, guilt, and insecurity just as in the nonassertive individual, only differently manifested. The aggressive individual may very well achieve his or her goal but, in the process of self-assertion, usually hurts others by making choices for them and minimizing their self-worth as persons. The assertive person is someone who acts in his own best interest, who stands up for himself without undue anxiety, who expresses his feelings comfortably, and who asserts his own rights without denying the rights of others. The assertive person will often achieve his goals and will usually feel good about himself. There is often room for others to achieve their goals as well in an assertive interaction (Alberti & Emmons, 1974).

The individual with generalized passive or aggressive behavior is the focus of this article. It is necessary to understand that everyone is situationally passive or aggressive because certain situations produce a great deal of anxiety. In such situations, one does not respond as adequately as one would like. The generalized nonassertive or aggressive person behaves timidly or with hostility in most situations. The behaviors are constant. Very few people can be assertive in all interactions, but everyone can increase the percentage of time and instances of assertiveness (Alberti & Emmons, 1974).

The following example of three different reactions to the same situation illustrates the three types of individuals. When a blind person is preparing to cross the street and a sighted pedestrian grabs the person's arm, offering to help him cross, the blind person could respond in at least one of three ways: 1) aggressively: by jerking his body away and angrily saying, "Leave me alone! I don't need anybody's help!" 2) passively: by meekly allowing the person to pull him across the street, wishing he would let go, but saying, "Well, I guess so...Okay, if you want to" or 3) assertively: by gently but firmly pulling his arm away and politely saying, "No, thank you. I appreciate your offer, but I can cross the street on my own and would prefer to do so." Similar situations with alternative responses have been generated by various authors, including Jakubowski-Spector (1973) and Phelps and Austin (1975). These situations can be adapted for blind or low vision individuals and can then be used as exercises in differentiating between passive, assertive, and aggressive behaviors.

An example of an adapted discrimination test in which the reader must choose which behavior is being portrayed follows:

1. Situation: Student gets silent instead of saying what is on his mind.
   Response: I guess you are uncomfortable talking about what's bothering you. I think we can work it out if you tell me what's irritating you.

2. Situation: You are talking to a rehabilitation counselor and you have been pressured to train for a vocation.
   Response: Well, okay, I guess that's pretty much what I was looking for. Yes, I suppose I'll work toward that job.

3. Situation: At a meeting, one person often interrupts you when you are speaking.
   Response: Excuse me. I would like to finish my statement.

4. Situation: A blind person approaches and asks you to purchase some materials.
   Response: You people think that just because you're blind, people have to buy stuff from you. Well, I'm certainly not going to!

5. Situation: You are having trouble writing a paper and don't know exactly what further information you need.

Response: I really must be dumb but I don't know where to begin on this paper.

6. Situation: The local library calls and asks you to return a book which you never checked out.
Response: What are you talking about? You people better get your records straight—I never had that book and don't try to make me pay for it.

(Answers: 1. assertive; 2. passive; 3. assertive; 4. aggressive; 5. passive; 6. aggressive.)

DEVELOPING AN ASSERTIVENESS PROGRAM

Awareness and exploration of feelings and development of non-verbal communication skills are at the foundation of assertion training (Phelps & Austin, 1975). The first step in this process is to increase an individual's awareness of the many feelings one experiences, such as loneliness, embarrassment, pride, guilt, confusion, shame, shyness, frustration, disgust, and reluctance. Techniques to foster this awareness can include reading paragraphs and stories and then discussing the feelings portrayed by the characters or observing and discussing pictures (possibly under the closed circuit television) portraying different gestures and facial expressions.

The next step in the process is to have individuals deal with their own feelings about themselves and about their visual disability. Feelings such as rejection, undesirableness, and anger can be explored through various techniques such as: *Magic Circle* (Ball, 1974): In this activity, children sit together in a circle. An affective question is posed, and each child is requested to answer the question. No other child seated may respond, either verbally or nonverbally, to the answer given, thus creating a nonthreatening environment for expression of feelings.

Journal writing: This technique can be utilized on a daily basis by both children and adults. Writing may be non-structured or responsive to a question given by the teacher or rehabilitation counselor, such as: What feelings do you experience when you enter an unfamiliar situation and no one approaches you?

Sentence completion: This method may be easier for some individuals than journal writing and can be used as a basis for oral discussions. Examples are: "When I am teased, I feel _____;

When I have to depend on other people to do things for me, I
_____; When I have to explain to others that I have low vision,
I tend to _____."

Role-playing: Create situations that the individual already has
had or may experience, and allow him or her to express the
feelings evoked.

Self-help groups: These groups may or may not deal with dis-
ability per se but would foster expression of feelings (i.e.,
Parents Without Partners, Alcoholics Anonymous, Diabetic
Support Group, etc.).

The Ungame (The Ungame Co., 1975): This board game sets
up situations and then has the player respond to a question
dealing with feelings or values in a safe environment.

Group or individual therapy sessions.

Interaction with other blind or low vision individuals: This contact can be particularly important for individuals who have little
or no interaction with other visually impaired persons (such as
a student in an itinerant program).

Exploring one's feelings associated with not being part of the
sighted or the blind world might give insight into the passive
behavior exhibited by some low vision individuals in their attempts
to "pass" as sighted. This expression of denial of the visual impairment creates a nonassertive stance in many situations in which
the visual problem might be revealed.

Once the individual is able to express feelings, one can delve
into the components of assertive behavior. Visually impaired persons, due to lack of visual feedback, might not be aware of the
message conveyed by their bodies. Five components include: 1)
gestures and facial expressions, 2) eye contact, 3) posture, 4)
voice, and 5) dress (Alberti & Emmons, 1974; Phelps & Austin,
1975).

Gestures can convey confidence and freedom and can emphasize the significance of what one is saying, for both negative and
positive feelings (Scheflen, 1972). A list of gestures and facial
expressions to be incorporated into a program on nonverbal communication is found below. Next to each action is the usual message conveyed.

Cocked head: attention; *lids narrowed*: suspicion, anger; *folding arms*: distance; *winks*: flirtation; *shrug shoulders*: perplexity;

hands on hip—thumb on belt loop: dominance; *eye avoidance*: inattention; *eyebrow flash*: recognition; *punch own palm*: emphatic; *nods head*: comprehension; *motioning gestures*: "Come here," "Go away," wave; *pointing gestures*: there, here, this, that, you, he, I; *descriptive gestures*: big, tiny, small, huge, large, round, flat, near, far, tall, short, long, wide, thick, narrow, straight, curved, rough, smooth, ordinal and cardinal numbers.

Methods to be used may include having the visually impaired individual feel the instructor's face and hands while demonstrating various gestures and expressions, physically motioning the visually impaired individual's body (including, but not limited to, the hands and face), and imitating gestures (making sure that the gestures are not made over-enthusiastically, which might be distracting). At this point, it is important to discuss the negative reaction which inappropriate behaviors, such as blindisms, elicit from the sighted (Apple, 1972; May, 1977). Once the visually impaired individual feels more competent in using the body in nonverbal communication, assignments can be given. Games may be played in which one person acts out an emotion, and the others must guess what emotion is being conveyed. Brailled or printed statements can be given to the student to be conveyed in a convincing manner, using proper body language. Examples of such statements which can be used as exercises for practicing gestures and facial expressions include:

- "Come over here and let me show you my new VersaBraille machine."

- "Gee, I don't have the answer to that question."

- "Go away from me right this minute—I don't want to talk about this anymore."

- "Absolutely not!"

- (With angry face) "That makes me so mad when you lie to me!"

- (With surprised face, after walking in on your birthday and all your friends yell "Surprise!") "Oh, my gosh!"

- (With face showing disgust) "I've really had it up to here—that's all I can take from you."

- (With worried face and furrowed brow) "I can't remember where I put my homework, and it's due next period."

- (With sad face) "That really hurt my feelings when you talked about me behind my back."
- (Waving with happy face) "Bye, it was really nice seeing you again. Come visit me again soon."

The second component, eye contact, is critical in showing interest and sincerity. Employment guides have stressed that eye contact is one of the primary factors considered during an interview (Mayo, 1975). When exploring this area, it is necessary to discuss habits which some partially sighted individuals have developed, such as staring, looking up and down at another person, and squinting while using peripheral vision. Although these gestures might increase one's visual perception, it is important to realize the reactions that might be elicited from others by these behaviors.

The next component, that of posture, shows self-confidence and interest in the other person (Scheflen, 1972). A blind or low vision individual, sitting with head down in class, in a meeting, or at a cultural event communicates boredom and disinterest, even if that is not the case. Correct posture development should be an integral part of the orientation and mobility program while working on body awareness and movement in space. Specific techniques to teach in role-playing situations include: walking with a confident stance; leaning toward the person speaking, but not too closely; facing the person speaking; and keeping one's head erect. These postures need to be reinforced as appropriate throughout the individual's daily life.

Visually impaired people are more aware of the impact of voice as an assertive component. Pitch, rate, tone, volume, stressed words, and quality of voice can communicate a variety of messages, such as assertiveness, confidence, sincerity, insecurity, passivity, and inferiority. A good technique to analyze one's voice is to tape the individual's normal voice and discuss how to make improvements. One should then practice with the tape recorder and seek feedback from significant others, such as parents, friends, and classmates.

The final component, dress, conveys an image. A favorite outfit can give one confidence, and vibrant colors can keep one from fading into the woodwork if one is shy or depressed. Appropriate dress and style of clothes are often what first impressions are based upon. These aspects of dress should be discussed openly and candidly. It may be appropriate to suggest having a color analysis done or seeking the advice of a fashion consultant.

All five components need to be addressed, and the effect they have on the sighted should be explained to the individual so that strategies for improving areas of weakness can be implemented. One strategy which has been shown to be effective is the use of a self-contract. The visually impaired individual contracts with him- or herself in writing and includes:

1. The specific changes he wants to make, deciding on realistic changes and manageable goals (i.e., if he wants to increase the amount of eye contact, then the first step might be to have eye contact with five people in a one-week period).

2. How she will monitor her progress (i.e., using a chart, a journal, or feedback from others).

3. How he will reward himself as he fulfills each part of the con-tract (i.e., buy a desired object, verbally praise himself, etc.).

4. What consequences will be imposed if she fails to meet the contract (i.e., not attending an upcoming event, depriving her-self of a wanted object, etc.).

ASSERTIVENESS TECHNIQUES

There are a variety of assertiveness techniques that can be learned and used singly or with other techniques of communica-tion. Some people may not be comfortable using certain tech-niques in specific situations, so the following techniques should be presented as options to the student or client to expand his/her repertoire of communication methods.

Role-playing can be used to practice all of the assertiveness techniques described in this article, as can the use of gestures and nonverbal communication techniques. It is helpful to choose meaningful situations for each student or client so that the practice can be seen as something which can be integrated into real-life sit-uations. Examples of situations for role-playing include: obtaining needed materials or services from a vocational counselor or gov-ernment worker; obtaining a booklist from next year's teachers; preparing for job interviews; initiating conversations; accepting and asking for dates; asking someone to dance; handling teasing; inviting peers to do activities outside of school; getting directions and sighted assistance on mobility lessons; phoning for bus information; shopping in stores; and refusing assistance when it is not needed. Follow-up with implementation of the learned skills in the actual situation is important once the individual feels comfortable in the simulated activities.

Initiating a Conversation

Many visually impaired people do not initiate conversations and often wait to be approached by others. Practicing techniques for reaching out to people and having successful interactions can be helpful. Five suggestions for a positive conversation are: 1) Identify yourself and your connection to the person you are talking to at the beginning of a conversation; 2) use "open" questions (how, why, etc.); 3) if one line of conversation seems to be going downhill, go back to something that was said earlier or go to a new topic; 4) offer information about yourself, and see if it is picked up, but do not monopolize the conversation with your problems and interests. Because others often focus on the problems of the visually impaired, blind or low vision individuals may tend to be egocentric in their conversation and might forget that others like talking about themselves, too; and 5) before parting, explore a commitment to meet again at a specified time and place. Set up an arrangement rather than wait for the other person to renew contact.

Broken Record Technique

The broken record technique can be used when responding to an unreasonable request, when a product or service is not satisfactory, or when being taken advantage of by another. The steps in using this technique are as follows:

- Get a clear picture of your goal. Know what it is that you want to accomplish.

- Make a clear statement of the goal.

- Keep repeating the message. Do not let it get distorted by old issues or side issues. Stay with the issue until it is resolved.

A situation in which a blind or low vision individual might use the broken record technique is when convincing a college counselor that a specific course is appropriate for the visually impaired student when meeting resistance for enrollment. This technique can be irritating if overused, so it should be used selectively. The person responding will generally run out of counter-arguments or will give up.

Content-Process Shift

Learning the difference between process and content during communication prevents one from being trapped by content issues and allows one to be in control of an interaction. The content-process shift can be used when the process message seems important or when it is interfering with the communication. Content refers to the statements made, opinions, responses, issues, etc. Process, on the other hand, refers to the feelings expressed—what you feel or perceive the other person is feeling. It is important to understand the two levels of communication and to try to be conscious of both levels so one can actively choose whether to stay with the content or to switch to the process. Many people get blocked in a conversation by continuing to focus on content when underlying feelings need to be openly expressed before proceeding with the content. For example, the blind student, when trying to get a booklist from a resistant teacher, may need to discuss the teacher's discomfort in having a blind person in his class before dealing with the issue of the booklist. Learning to separate these two levels of communication is an invaluable tool in many interactions.

Handling Anger

Your Anger

Anger can often sabotage effective communication and keep one from achieving one's goal. It is important to learn how to express angry feelings without hurting someone physically or emotionally in the process. Some positive ways to express anger are: 1) with a physical expression of strong feelings before or after a situation such as hitting a pillow, hitting with a bataka bat, stomping the floor, banging the table, exercising, crying, etc.; 2) with a verbal expression of anger in direct statements, such as "I am very angry!" or "I strongly disagree with you!"; 3) writing about the anger before or after a situation to vent the feelings; or 4) going to a "time-out" or "cool-down" place to think about or express angry feelings alone.

Disarming Others' Anger

There are many times when one encounters another person's anger in an interaction. It is important to have techniques available for disarming someone else's angry feelings. In interpersonal relationships, one is most effective by: 1) acknowledging the anger by saying, "Okay, I understand you are angry," and avoiding defensive statements which could escalate the situation; 2) staying calm and expressing the desire to problem-solve the situation with statements such as "I hear you are really angry. I would like to talk about it. Let's sit down and discuss your feelings"; 3) trying to lower the tension level, trying to resolve the issue, and trying not to placate the other person.

In some situations, particularly with authority figures such as teachers, counselors, bosses, etc., the use of negative inquiry can be very effective in disarming another person's anger. Negative inquiry involves the following steps: 1) Clarify the message you are receiving by repeating what you think you have heard with statements such as "Let me see if I got it. You are angry that I ..." or "You feel I haven't come through by..."; 2) Ask for further feedback with statements such as "Is there anything else that is bothering you?"; 3) Continue asking questions until the tension is reduced, and try to avoid conflict. These anger-disarming techniques are useful tools for creating a cooling down period and allowing a meaningful interaction to continue.

EFFECTIVE ASSERTIVE STATEMENTS

Sometimes, the way a need or feeling is expressed makes a significant impact on others. There are many examples of effective assertive statements which can create a feeling of control over one's life. By using a clear and direct approach in communication, many hidden messages can be eliminated and more needs can be met. The following illustrations show situations in which effective assertive statements can be made. 1) When you want to ask for time or distance, say "I need to think about that one for awhile" or "I need more information before I make a decision." 2) When you need to obtain a commitment from someone, say "Then I am to understand that you will _____" or "When can you give me a firm answer?" 3) When you want to make sure the receiver is getting your message, say "This is what I need: a) _____, b) _____, c) _____" or "I want to make clear the point that _____" 4) When you want to make sure you are receiving the message, say "Let me see if I got it _____ what you want is _____" or "I am confused; please tell me again." 5) When you want to share a positive feeling, say "I really like the way you _____" or "I am glad to see that you _____" 6) When you are feeling uncomfortable or upset, say "Before we go on, I want to tell you I am uncomfortable with _____" or "I get embarrassed when _____."

COMPLETE COMMUNICATION

There are six steps that are important to learn and practice before entering into an anxiety-producing situation. The steps in complete communication should be taken so that one feels in control. The steps to consider and develop in role-playing situations are as follows:

1. Decide what your goal is beforehand. What message do you want the other person to receive?

2. How do you feel about telling the other person this message? Identify your own feelings (i.e., afraid, nervous, fearful of rejection, embarrassed, etc.).

3. What are your fears or fantasies about the other person if you tell them this message?

4. What are the possible outcomes?

5. What are the alternative responses you can make to the possible outcomes?

6. Stay focused and stick to the subject.

CONCLUSION

The role of the teacher and rehabilitation counselor in providing alternative techniques for effective communication is critical for the reduction of passive and aggressive behaviors and in the development of more assertive blind and partially sighted individuals. The education and rehabilitation settings should offer an array of options for improving communication techniques so that interpersonal relationships are more meaningful and enduring and so that the opportunities for success in the world of work are increased. By feeling more in control of one's environment, the assertive visually impaired person has a better self-concept and is more in charge of the direction his/her life takes. Moreover, acquiring and using verbal and nonverbal assertiveness and communication skills will enable the individual to move more smoothly into the mainstream of society.

References
and Readings

References

Adelson, E. (1983). Precursors of early language development in children born blind from birth. In A. Mills (Ed.), *Language acquisition in the blind child* (pp. 1–12). San Diego College-Hill Press.

Agar, M. H. (1980). *The professional stranger: An introduction to ethnography.* New York: Academic Press.

Alberti, R. E., & Emmons, M. L. (1974). *Your perfect right: A guide to assertive behavior.* San Luis Obispo, CA: Impact.

Allport, G. W. (1958). *The nature of prejudice.* Garden City, NY: Doubleday Anchor Books.

Als, H. (1982). The unfolding of behavioral organization in the face of a biological violation. In E. Tronick (Ed.), *Social interchange in infancy: Affect, cognition, and communication* (pp. 125–160). Baltimore: University Park Press.

Andersen, E. S., Dunlea, A., & Kekelis, L. S. (1984). Blind children's language: Resolving some differences. *Journal of Child Language, 11,* 645–664.

Andersen, E. S., & Kekelis, L. S. (1982, October). *The effects of visual impairment on early mother-child interactions.* Paper presented at the Seventh Annual Conference on Child Development, Boston University.

Andersen, E. S., & Kekelis, L. S. (1983, October). *The role of children in determining their linguistic input.* Paper presented at the Eighth Annual Conference on Child Language Development, Boston University.

Andersen, E. S., & Kekelis, L. S. (1984, May). *The role of visual perception in conversational interaction.* Paper presented at the International Communication Association Conference, San Francisco.

Andersen, E. S., & Kekelis, L. S. (1985, March). *Language input and language acquisition: Evidence from special populations.* Paper presented at the 17th Annual Child Language Research Forum, Stanford University, Stanford, CA.

Andersen, E. S., & Kekelis, L. S. (1986). The role of sibling input in the language socialization of younger blind children. *Southern California occasional papers in linguistics, Vol. 11: Social and cognitive perspectives on language* (pp. 141–156). Los Angeles: University of Southern California Press.

Andersen, E. S., Kekelis, L. S., & McGinnis, M. (1984, October). *The contribution of sibling/peer input to the language development of blind children.* Paper presented at the Ninth Annual Child Language Conference, Boston University.

Apple, M. M. (1972). Kinesic training for blind persons: A vital means of communication. *New Outlook for the Blind, 66,* 201–208.

Argyle, M. (1980). Interaction skills and social competence. In P. Feldman & J. Orford (Eds.), *Psychological problems: The social context* (pp. 123–150). Chichester, England: John Wiley & Sons.

Argyle, M., & Kendon, A. (1967). The experimental analysis of social performance. In L. Berkowitz (Ed.), *Advances in experimental social psychology* (Vol. 3, pp. 58–98). New York: Academic Press.

Asher, S. R., & Gottman, J. M. (1981). *The development of children's friendships.* Cambridge, England: Cambridge University Press.

Asher, S. R., Oden, S. L., & Gottman, J. M. (1977). Children's friendships in social settings. In L. G. Katz (Ed.), *Current topics in early childhood* (Vol. 1, pp. 33–61). Norwood, NJ: Ablex.

Axelrod, S. (1959). *Effects of early blindness: Performance of blind and sighted children on tactile and auditory tasks* (Research Report No. 7). New York: American Foundation for the Blind.

Ball, G. (1974). *Magic circle: An overview of the human development program.* La Mesa, CA: Human Development Training Institute.

Bandura, A. (1977). *Social learning theory.* Englewood Cliffs, NJ: Prentice-Hall.

Bandura, A., & Walters, R. H. (1963). *Social learning and personality development.* New York: Holt, Rinehart & Winston.

Bateman, B. (1965). Psychological evaluation of blind children. *New Outlook for the Blind, 59,* 193–196.

Bates, P., Morron, S. A., Pancsofar, E., & Sedlak, R. (1984). The effect of functional vs. non-functional activities on attitudes/expectations of non-handicapped college students: What they see is what we get. *Journal of the Association for Persons with Severe Handicaps, 9*(2), 73–78.

Bateson, G. (1944). Cultural determinants of personality. In I. J. McVickers Hunt (Ed.), *Personality and the behavior disorders*, Vol. 2. New York: Royal Press.

Bellack, A. S. (1983). Recurrent problems in the behavioral assessment of social skill. *Behavior Research Therapy, 21,* 29–41.

Bellack, A. S., Hersen, M., & Turner, S. M. (1978). Role play tests for assessing social skills: Are they valid? *Behavior Therapy, 9,* 448–461.

Bianchi, B. D., & Bakeman, R. (1978). Sex-typed preferences observed in preschoolers: Traditional and open school differences. *Child Development, 49,* 910–912.

Bishop, V.E. (1986). Identifying the components of successful mainstreaming. *Journal of Visual Impairment & Blindness, 80,* 939–946.

Bonney, M.E. (1971). Assessment of efforts to aid socially isolated elementary school pupils. *Journal of Educational Research, 64,* 345–364.

Borman, K. M. (1979). Children's situational competence: Two studies. In O. K. Garnica & M. L. King (Eds.), *Language, children and society* (pp. 81–113). New York: Pergamon Press.

Bullis, M., & Gaylord-Ross, R. (1991). *Moving on: Transitions for youth with behavioral disorders.* Reston, VA: Council for Exceptional Children.

Burlingham, D. (1965). Some problems of ego development in blind children. *Psychoanalytic Study of the Child, 20,* 194–208.

Centers, L., & Centers, R. (1963). Peer group attitudes toward the amputee child. *Journal of Social Psychology, 61,* 127–132.

Charlesworth, R., & Hartup, W. W. (1967). Positive social reinforcement in the nursery school peer group. *Child Development, 38,* 993–1002.

Chernus-Mansfield, N., Hayashi, D., Horn, M., & Kekelis, L. S. (1985).

Heart to heart: Parents of blind children talk about their feelings. Los Angeles: Blind Childrens Center.

Chernus-Mansfield, N., Hayashi, D., & Kekelis, L. S. (1985). *Talk to me II: Common concerns.* Los Angeles: Blind Childrens Center.

Chin-Perez, G., Hartman, D., Sook Park, H., Sacks, S., Wershing, A., & Gaylord-Ross, R. J. (1986). Maximizing social contact for secondary students with severe handicaps. *Journal of the Association for Persons with Severe Handicaps, 11*, 118–124.

Clark, L., & Warren, D. (1978). Sensory awareness. *Journal of Visual Impairment & Blindness, 72*, 333–334.

Coie, J. D., & Kupersmidt, J. B. (1983). A behavioral analysis of emerging social status in boys' groups. *Child Development, 54*, 1400–1416.

Cook-Gumperz, J., & Corsaro, W. (1977). Social-ecological constraints on children's communicative strategies. *Sociology, 11*, 411–434.

Coopersmith, S. (1967). *Antecedents of self-esteem.* San Francisco: W. H. Freeman.

Corsaro, W. A. (1979). "We're friends, right?" Children's use of access rituals in a nursery school. *Language in Society, 8*, 411–434.

Corsaro, W. A. (1985). *Friendship and peer culture in the early years.* Norwood, NJ: Ablex.

Cowen, E. L., Petersen, A., Babigian, H., Izzo, L. D., & Trost, M. A. (1973). Long-term follow-up of early detected vulnerable children. *Journal of Consulting and Clinical Psychology, 41*, 438–445.

Curry, S. A., & Hatlen, P. H. (1988). Meeting the unique educational needs of visually impaired pupils through appropriate placement. *Journal of Visual Impairment & Blindness, 82*, 417–424.

Davies, B. (1982). *Life in the classroom and playground: The accounts of primary school children.* Boston: Routledge & Kegan Paul.

DeVries, D. L., & Edwards, K. J. (1974). Student teams and learning games: Their effects on cross-race and cross-sex interaction. *Journal of Educational Psychology, 66*, 741–749.

Dinkmeyer, D. (1970). *Developing an understanding of self and others (DUSO).* Circle Pines, MN: American Guidance Service.

Dion, K. K. (1972). Physical attractiveness and evaluation of children's transgressions. *Journal of Personality and Social Development, 24*, 207–213.

Dion, K. K., Berscheid, E., & Walster, E. (1972). What is beautiful is good. *Journal of Personality and Social Psychology, 24*, 285–290.

Dobbert, M. L. (1982). *Ethnographic research: Theory and application for modern schools and society.* New York: Praeger.

Dodge, K. A. (1983). Behavioral antecedents of peer social status. *Child Development, 54*, 1386–1399.

Duehl, A. (1979). The effects of creative dance movement on large muscle control and balance of congenitally blind children. *Journal of Visual Impairment & Blindness, 73*, 127–133.

Dunlea, A. (1989). *Vision and the emergence of meaning: Blind and sighted children's early language.* Cambridge, England: Cambridge University Press.

Durkheim, E. (1973). *Moral education: A study in the theory and application of the sociology of education* (E. K. Wilson & H. Schnurer, Trans.). New York: Free Press. (Original work published 1925)

Eagelstein, S. A. (1975). The social acceptance of blind high school students in an integrated school. *New Outlook for the Blind, 69*, 447–451.

Eckerman, C. O., & Whately, J. L. (1977). Toys and special interaction between infant peers. *Child Development, 48,* 1645–1656.

Epstein, J. L. (1986). Friendship selection: Developmental and environmental influences. In E. C. Mueller & C. R. Cooper (Eds.), *Process and outcome in peer relationships* (pp. 129–160). New York: Academic Press.

Erikson, E. H. (1950). *Childhood and society.* New York: W. W. Norton.

Erin, J. N. (1986). Frequencies and types of questions in the language of visually impaired children. *Journal of Visual Impairment & Blindness, 80,* 670–674.

Farkas, G. M., Sherick, R., Matson, J. L., & Loebig, M. (1981). Skills training of a blind child via differential reinforcement. *Behavior Therapist, 4,* 24–26.

Fine, G. A. (1981). Friends, impression management and preadolescent behavior. In S. R. Asher & J. M. Gottman (Eds.), *The development of children's friendships* (pp. 29–52). Cambridge, England: Cambridge University Press.

Flyegelman, A. (Ed.). (1976). *The New Games Book.* Garden City, NY: Dolphin Books.

Foster, S. L., & Richey, W. L. (1979). Issues in the assessment of social competence in children. *Journal of Applied Behavior Analysis, 12,* 625–638.

Fraiberg, S. (1977). *Insights from the blind.* New York: Basic Books.

Fredericks, H. B., Baldwin, V., Grove, D., Moore, W., Riggs, C., & Lyons, B. (1978). Integrating the moderately and severely handicapped child into a normal day care setting. In M. J. Guralnick (Ed.), *Early intervention and the integration of handicapped and nonhandicapped children* (191–206). Baltimore: University Park Press.

Freud, S. (1974). Three essays on the theory of sexuality. In J. Strachey (Ed. and Trans.), *The standard edition of the complete psychological works of Sigmund Freud* (Vol. 7, pp. 123–231). London: Hogarth Press. (Original work published 1905)

Freud, S. (1974). The dissolution of the Oedipus complex. In J. Strachey (Ed. and Trans.), *The standard edition of the complete psychological works of Sigmund Freud* (Vol. 19, pp. 173–182). London: Hogarth Press. (Original work published 1924)

Freud, S. (1974). Civilization and its discontents. In J. Strachey (Ed. and Trans.), *The standard edition of the complete psychological works of Sigmund Freud* (Vol. 21, pp. 64–145). London: Hogarth Press. (Original work published 1930)

Friedman, C. T. (1986). *Interaction and attachment: Determinants of individual differences in a sample of visually impaired one-and two-year-olds and their mothers.* Unpublished doctoral dissertation, University of California, Berkeley.

Gall, R. S. (1987). Framework for policy and action in special education and international perspective in the future of special education. In *Proceedings of the CEC Symposium.* Reston, VA: Council for Exceptional Children.

Garnica, O. K. (1981). Social dominance and conversational interaction—The omega child in the classroom. In J. L. Green & C. Wallat (Eds.), *Ethnography and language in educational settings* (pp. 229–252). Norwood, NJ: Ablex.

Garvey, C. (1977). Play with language and speech. In S. Ervin-Tripp & C.

Mitchell-Kernan (Eds.), *Child discourse* (pp. 27–47). New York: Academic Press.

Gaylord-Ross, R. J., Haring, T. G., Breen, C. G., & Pitts-Conway, V. (1984). The training and generalization of social interaction skills with autistic youth. *Journal of Applied Behavior Analysis, 17,* 229–247.

Gaylord-Ross, R. J., & Holvoet, J. F. (1985). *Strategies for educating students with severe handicaps.* Boston: Little Brown.

Gaylord-Ross, R. J., & Pitts-Conway, V. (1984). Social behavior development in integrated secondary autistic programs. In N. Certo, N. Haring, & R. York (Eds.), *Public school integration of severely handicapped students: Rational issues and progressive alternatives* (pp. 197–219). Baltimore: Paul H. Brookes.

Glassner, B. (1976). Kid society. *Urban Education, 11,* 5–22.

Gottlieb, J., & Budoff, M. (1973). Social acceptability of retarded children in nongraded schools differing in architecture. *American Journal of Mental Deficiency, 78,* 15–19.

Gottlieb, J., Semmel, M. L., & Veldman, D. J. (1978). Correlates of social status among mainstreamed retarded children. *Journal of Educational Psychology, 70,* 396–405.

Gottman, J., Gonso. J., & Rasmussen, B. (1975). Social interaction, social competence, and friendship in children. *Child Development, 46,* 709–718.

Gresham, F. M. (1981). Social skills training with handicapped children: A review. *Review of Educational Research, 51,* 139–176.

Gresham, F. M. (1982). Misguided mainstreaming: The case for social skills training with handicapped children. *Exceptional Children, 48,* 422–433.

Hallinan, M. T. (1976). Friendship patterns in open and traditional classrooms. *Sociology of Education, 49,* 254–264.

Hallinan, M. T. (1979). Structural effects on children's friendships and cliques. *Social Psychology Quarterly, 42,* 43–54.

Hammersley, M., & Woods, P. (Eds.). (1984). *Life in school: The sociology of pupil culture.* Milton Keynes, England: Open University Press.

Harlow, H. F., & Harlow, M. K. (1962). Social deprivation in monkeys. *Scientific American, 207*(5), 1–10.

Harrell, R. L., & Curry, S. A. (1987). Services to blind and visually impaired children and adults: Who is responsible? *Journal of Visual Impairment & Blindness, 81,* 368–376.

Harrell, R. L., & Strauss, F. A. (1986). Approaches to increasing assertive behavior and communication skills in blind and visually impaired persons. *Journal of Visual Impairment & Blindness, 80,* 794–798.

Harter, S. (1979). *Perceived competence scale for children (PCSC).* Boulder: Department of Counseling, University of Colorado.

Harter, S. (1982). The perceived competence scale for children. *Child Development, 53,* 87–97.

Hartup, W. W. (1977). Peer interaction and the process of socialization. In M. J. Guralnick (Ed.), *Early intervention and interaction of handicapped and nonhandicapped children* (pp. 27–51). Baltimore: University Park Press.

Hartup, W. W., Glazer, J. A., & Charlesworth, R. (1967). Peer reinforcement and sociometric status. *Child Development, 38,* 1017–1024.

Hatch, J. A. (1984). Peer interaction and the development of social competence. *Child Study Journal, 17,* 169–183.

Hatlen, P. H. (1980). Mainstreaming: Origin of a concept. *Blindness* (Annual, American Association of Workers for the Blind, Washington, DC), 1–8.

Hatlen, P. H., & Curry, S. A. (1987). In support of specialized programs for blind and visually impaired children: The impact of visual loss on learning. *Journal of Visual Impairment & Blindness, 81,* 7–13.

Hersen, M., & Bellack, A. (1977). Assessment of social skills. In A. Ciminero, K. Calhoun, & H. Adams (Eds.), *Handbook for behavioral assessment* (pp. 509–554). New York: John Wiley & Sons.

Hertz-Lazarowitz, R., Sharan, S., & Steinberg, R. (1980). Classroom learning style and cooperative behavior of elementary school children. *Journal of Educational Psychology, 72,* 99–106.

Hinshaw, S. P., Henker, B., & Whalen, C. K. (1984). Self-control in hyperactive boys in anger-inducing situations: Effects of cognitive-behavior training and of methylphenidate. *Journal of Abnormal Child Psychology, 12,* 55–77.

Hoben, M., & Lindstrom, V. (1980). Evidence of isolation in the mainstream. *Journal of Visual Impairment & Blindness, 74,* 289–292.

Imamura, S. (1965). *Mother and blind child.* New York: American Foundation for the Blind.

Innocenti, M. S., Stowitschek, J. J., Rule, S., Killoran, J., Striefel, S., & Boswell, C. (1986). A naturalistic study of the relation between preschool setting events and peer interaction in four activity contexts. *Early Childhood Research Quarterly, 1,* 141–153.

Jakubowski-Spector, P. A. (1973). Facilitating the growth of women through assertion training. *Counseling Psychologist, 4*(1), 77.

Johnson, R. T., & Johnson, D. W. (1981). Building friendships between handicapped and non-handicapped children: Effects of cooperative and individualistic instruction. *American Educational Research Journal, 18,* 415–423.

Jones, R. L., & Chiba, C. (1985). *Social skills assessment and intervention* (Final report). Bethesda, MD: National Institute of Child Health and Human Development.

Jones, R. L., Lavine, K., & Shell, J. (1972). Blind children integrated in classrooms with sighted children: A sociometric study. *New Outlook for the Blind, 66,* 75–80.

Kazdin, A. E. (1982). *Single-case research designs: Methods for clinical and applied settings.* Baltimore: University Park Press.

Kekelis, L. S. (1981). *Mothers' input to blind children.* Unpublished master's thesis, University of Southern California, Los Angeles.

Kekelis, L. S. (1986a). *Increasing positive social interactions between a blind child and sighted kindergartners.* Unpublished paper, San Francisco State University, San Francisco.

Kekelis, L. S. (1986b). [Pilot study of a blind child's social interactions]. Unpublished raw data.

Kekelis, L. S. (1988a). Case study of a blind child in two school settings. In S. Z. Sacks, L. S. Kekelis, & R. J. Gaylord-Ross (Eds.), *The development of social skills by visually impaired children.* San Francisco: San Francisco State University.

Kekelis, L. S. (1988b). Increasing positive social interactions between a blind child and sighted kindergartners. In S. Z. Sacks, L. S. Kekelis, & R. J. Gaylord-Ross (Eds.), *The development of social skills by visually impaired children.* San Francisco: San Francisco State University.

Kekelis, L. S., & Andersen, E. S. (1984). Family communication styles and language development. *Journal of Visual Impairment & Blindness, 78,* 54–65.

Kekelis, L. S., & Chernus-Mansfield, N. (1984). *Talk to me: A language guide for parents of blind children.* Los Angeles: Blind Childrens Center.

Kekelis, L. S., & Sacks, S. Z. (1988). Mainstreaming visually impaired children into regular education programs: The effects of visual impairment on children's interactions with peers. In S. Z. Sacks, L. S. Kekelis, & R. J. Gaylord-Ross (Eds.), *The development of social skills by visually impaired children.* San Francisco: San Francisco State University.

Kelly, J.A. (1982). *Social skills training: A practical guide for interventions.* New York: Springer.

Kleck, R. E. (1968). Physical stigma and non-verbal cues emitted in face to face interactions. *Human Relations, 21,* 19–28.

Kohlberg, L. (1969). Stages and sequence: The cognitive development approach to socialization. In D. A. Goslin (Ed.), *Handbook of socialization theory and research.* Chicago: Rand McNally.

La Greca, A. M., & Start, P. (1986). Naturalistic observation of children's social behavior. In P. S. Strain, M. J. Guralnick, & H. M. Walker (Eds.), *Children's social behavior: Development, assessment, and modification* (pp. 181–213). New York: Academic Press.

Langlois, J. H., & Downs, A. C. (1979). Peer relations as a function of physical attractiveness: The eye of the beholder or behavioral reality? *Child Development, 50,* 409–418.

Lieberman, A. F. (1977). Preschoolers' competence with a peer: Relations with attachment and peer experience. *Child Development, 48,* 1277–1287.

Mangold, S. (1980). Nurturing high self-esteem in visually handicapped children. In T. D. Yawley (Ed.), *The self concept of the young child.* Provo, UT: Brigham Young University.

Marascuilo, L. A., & Busk, P. L. (1985). *Combining statistics for multiple subjects in single-subject research.* Paper presented at the annual meeting of the American Educational Research Association, Chicago.

May, M. (1977). *AFB practice report: Nonverbal communication and the congenitally blind: A subject bibliography of print and non-print materials for the development of training programs.* New York: American Foundation for the Blind.

Mayo, G. (1975). *Use of eye contact by blind persons as a means of increasing communication during an employment interview.* Unpublished doctoral dissertation, University of Arizona, Tucson.

McFall, R. M. (1982). A review and reformulation of the concept of social skills. *Behavior Assessment, 4,* 1–33.

McGuinnes, R. M. (1970). A descriptive study of blind children educated in the itinerant teacher, resource room and special school setting. *Research Bulletin, American Foundation for the Blind, 20,* 1–56.

Meichenbaum, D. H. (1977). *Cognitive behavior modification: An integrative approach.* New York: Plenum Press.

Meyer, G. F. (1929).Some advantages offered children in day school classes for the blind in the public schools. *Outlook for the Blind, 22*(4), 9–15.

Mischel, W. (1966). A social learning view of sex differences in behavior. In E. E. Maccoby (Ed.), *The development of sex differences.* Palo Alto, CA: Stanford University Press.

Moore, S.G. (1967). Correlates of peer acceptance in nursery school children. In W.W. Hartup & N. L. Smothergill (Eds.), *The young child* (pp. 56–81). Washington, DC: National Association for the Education of Young Children.

Mueller, E. (1972). The maintenance of verbal exchanges between young children. *Child Development, 43,* 930–938.

Mueller, E., & Brenner, J. (1977). The origins of social skills and interaction among playgroup toddlers. *Child Development, 48,* 854–861.

Mueller, E., & Rich, A. (1976). Clustering and socially-directed behaviors in a playgroup of 1-year-old boys. *Journal of Child Psychology and Psychiatry, 17,* 315–322.

Mulford, R. (1983). Referential development in blind children. In A. E. Mills (Ed.), *Language acquisition in the blind child* (pp. 89–107). San Diego: College-Hill Press.

Naughton, F., & Sacks, S. Z. (1977). *Hey! What's cooking? A kitchen curriculum for parents of visually handicapped children.* Flosmoor, IL: South Metropolitan Association for Low Incidence Handicapped Children.

Nucci, L., & Turiel, E. (1978). Social interactions and development of social concepts in pre-school children. *Child Development, 49,* 400–408.

Park, H. S. & Gaylord-Ross, R. J. (1989). A problem-solving approach to social skills training in employment settings with mentally retarded youth. *Journal of Applied Behavior Analysis, 22,* 373–380.

Park, H. S., Marascuilo, L., & Gaylord-Ross, R. J. (1987). *Visual inspection versus statistical analysis in single case data.* Unpublished manuscript, San Francisco State University.

Parsons, S. (1986). Function of play in low vision children. Part 2: Emerging patterns of behavior. *Journal of Visual Impairment & Blindness, 80,* 777–784.

Petersen, G. A., Austin, G. J., & Lang, R. P. (1979). Use of teacher prompts to increase social behavior: Generalization effects with severely and profoundly retarded adolescents. *American Journal of Mental Deficiency, 84,* 82–86.

Petrucci, D. (1953). The blind child and his adjustment. *New Outlook for the Blind, 47,* 240–246.

Phelps, S., & Austin, N. (1975). *The assertive woman.* San Luis Obispo, CA: Impact.

Piaget, J. (1959). *The language and thought of the child* (M. Gabain, Trans.). New York: Humanities Press. (Original work published 1926)

Piaget, J. (1965). *The moral judgment of the child* (M. Gabain, Trans.). New York: Free Press. (Original work published 1932)

Pollard, A. (1985). *The social world of the primary school.* Eastbourne, England: Holt, Rinehart, & Winston.

Prizant, B. M. (1987). Toward an understanding of verbal repetition in the language of visually-impaired children. *Australian Journal of Human Communication Disorders, 15,* 79–90.

Putallaz, M., & Gottman, J. M. (1979). *An interactional model of children's entry into peer groups.* Unpublished manuscript, University of Illinois, Urbana-Champaign.

Putallaz, M., & Gottman, J. M. (1981). Social skills and group acceptance. In S. R. Asher & J. M. Gottman (Eds.), *The development of children's friendships* (pp. 116–149). New York: Cambridge University Press.

Putallaz, M., & Gottman, J. M. (1982). Conceptualizing social competence in children. In P. Karoly & J. J. Steffen (Eds.), *Improving children's competence* (pp. 1–33). Lexington, MA: Lexington Books.

Quintal, J. (1986). How are we doing? Issues and research related to the integration of students with special needs. *Proceedings of the Canadian Symposium on Special Education* (pp. A, 1–13). Toronto: Ontario Council of Administrators of Special Education.

Raver, S. A., & Drash, P. W. (1988). Increasing social skills training for visually impaired children. *Education of the Visually Handicapped, 19,* 147–155.

Reardon, M. P., & Sacks, S. Z. (1985). *Social skills training: Foundation for functional learning.* Paper presented at the meeting of California Transcribers and Educators of the Visually Handicapped, San Francisco.

Rickelman, B. L., & Blaylock, J. N. (1983). Behaviors of sighted individuals perceived by blind persons as hindrances to self-reliance in blind persons. *Journal of Visual Impairment & Blindness, 77,* 8–11.

Roessing, L. J. (1983). Methods of teaching low vision children (Unpublished papers, Vols. 1, 2, and 3). San Francisco State University, San Francisco.

Roff, M., Sells, S. G., & Golden, M. M. (1972). *Social adjustment and personality development in children.* Minneapolis: University of Minnesota Press.

Rogow, S. (1975). Perceptual organization in blind children. *New Outlook for the Blind, 78,* 226–233.

Rowland, C. (1984). Preverbal communication of blind infants and their mothers. *Journal of Visual Impairment & Blindness, 78,* 297–302.

Rubin, Z. (1980). *Children's friendships.* Cambridge, MA: Harvard University Press.

Sackin, S., & Thelan, E. (1984). An ethological study of peaceful associative outcomes to conflict in preschool children. *Child Development, 55,* 1098–1102.

Sacks, S. Z. (1987). *Peer-mediated social skills training: Enhancing the social competence of visually handicapped children in a mainstream school setting.* Unpublished doctoral dissertation, University of California, Berkeley, and San Francisco State University, San Francisco.

Sacks, S. Z., & Gaylord-Ross, R. J. (1989). Peer-mediated and teacher-directed social skills training for visually impaired students. *Behavior Therapy, 20,* 619–638.

Sacks, S., & Reardon, M. P. (1989). Maximizing social interaction for students with visual handicaps. In R. Gaylord-Ross (Ed.), *Integration strategies for students with handicaps* (pp. 77–104). Baltimore: Paul H. Brookes.

Sacks, S., Russell, D., Hirsch, M., Braden, J., & Gaylord-Ross, R. (1991). *Social skills training: What professionals say they do.* Submitted for publication.

Sanders, R. M., & Goldberg, S. G. (1977). Eye contact: Increasing their rate in social interactions. *Journal of Visual Impairment & Blindness, 71,* 265–267.

Sandler, A. M. (1963). Aspects of passivity and ego development in the blind infant. *Psychoanalytic Study of the Child, 18,* 343–361.

Santa Clara Unified School District. (1980). Project esteem. Santa Clara, CA: Author.

Santin, S., & Nesker-Simmons, J. (1977). Problems in the construction of reality in congenitally blind children. *Journal of Visual Impairment & Blindness, 71,* 425–429.

Schatzman, L., & Strauss, A. L. (1973). *Field research: Strategies for a natural sociology.* Englewood Cliffs, NJ: Prentice-Hall.

Scheflen, A. E. (1972). *Body language and social order communication as behavioral control.* Englewood Cliffs, NJ: Prentice-Hall.

Schein, E. H. (1985). *Organizational culture and leadership.* San Francisco: Jossey-Bass.

Scott, R. A. (1969a). The socialization of blind children. In D. A. Goslin (Ed.),*Handbook of socialization theory and research* (pp. 1025–1045). Chicago: Rand McNally.

Scott, R. A. (1969b). *The making of blind men: A study of adult socialization.* New York: Russell Sage Foundation.

Sears, R. (1957). Identification of a form of behavioral development. In I. D. B. Harris (Ed.), *The concept of development.* Minneapolis: University of Minnesota Press.

Seligman, M. (1975). *Helplessness on depression, development, and death.* San Francisco: W. H. Freeman.

Shantz, D. W. (1986). Conflict, aggression, and peer status: An observational study. *Child Development, 57,* 1322–1332.

Shure, M. B. (1963). Psychological ecology of a nursery school. *Child Development, 34,* 979–992.

Sisson, L. A., Van Hasselt, V. B., Hersen, M., & Strain, P. (1985). Increasing social behavior in multihandicapped children through peer interaction. *Behavior Modification, 9,* 293–321.

Snow, C. E., & Ferguson, C. A. (1977). *Talking to children.* New York: Cambridge University Press.

Spradley, J. P. (1980). *Participant observation.* New York: Holt, Rinehart, & Winston.

Stamback, M., & Verba, M. (1986). Organization of social play among toddlers: An ecological approach. In E. C. Mueller & C. R. Cooper (Eds.), *Process and outcome in peer relationships* (pp. 229–247). New York: Academic Press.

Stokes, T. R., & Baer, D. M. (1977). An implicit technology of generalization. *Journal of Applied Behavior Analysis, 7,* 349–367.

Strain, P. S., Cooke, T. P., & Apolloni, T. (1976). *Teaching exceptional children: Assessing and modifying social behavior.* New York: Academic Press.

Strain, P. S., & Kohler, F. W. (1988). Social skill intervention with young children with handicaps: Some new conceptualizations and directions. In S. Odom & M. Karnes (Eds.), *Early intervention for infants and children with handicaps: An empirical base* (pp. 129–143). Baltimore: Paul H. Brookes.

Strain, P. S., & Odom, S. L. (1986). Peer social initiations: Effective intervention for social skills development of exceptional children. *Exceptional Children, 52,* 543–551.

Sullivan, H. S. (1953). *The interpersonal theory of psychiatry.* New York: W. W. Norton.

Tait, P. (1972). The effects of circumstantial rejection in infant behavior. *New Outlook for the Blind, 66,* 139–151.

Tillman, M, & Williams H. (1967). The performances of blind and sighted children on the Wechsler Intelligence Scale for Children, study II. *International Journal for Education of the Blind, 16,* 106–112.

Trower, P. (1982). Toward a generative model of social skills: A critique and synthesis. In J. P. Curran & P. M. Monti (Eds.), *Social skills training.* New York: Guilford Press.

Ungame Co. (1975). *Tell it like it is with the Ungame.* Anaheim, CA: Author.

Urwin, C. (1983). Dialogue and cognitive functioning in the early language development of three blind children. In A. Mills (Ed.), *Language acquisition in the blind child* (pp. 142–161). San Diego: College-Hill Press.

Van Hasselt, V. B. (1983a). Social adaptation in the blind. Clinical *Psychology Review,* 3,87–102.

Van Hasselt, V. B. (1983b). Visual impairment. In M. R. Hersen, V. B. Van Hasselt, & J. L. Matson (Eds.), *Behavior therapy for the developmentally and physically disabled* (pp. 109–129). New York: Academic Press.

Van Hasselt, V. B., Hersen, M., & Kazdin, A. E. (1984). Assessment of social skills in visually handicapped adolescents. *Behaviour Research and Therapy, 22,* 689–696.

Van Hasselt, V. B., Hersen, M., Kazdin, A. E., Simon, J .A., & Mastanuono, A. K. (1982). *A behavior-analytic model for assessing social skills in blind adolescents.* Paper presented at the annual convention of the Association for the Advancement of Behavior Therapy, Toronto.

Van Hasselt, V. B., Hersen, M., Kazdin, A. E., Simon, J. A., & Mastanuono, A. K. (1983). Social skills training for blind adolescents. *Journal of Visual Impairment & Blindness, 77,* 99–103.

Vandell, D. L., Wilson, K. S., & Buchanan, N. R. (1980). Peer interaction in the first year of life: An examination of its structure, content, and sensitivity to toys. *Child Development, 51,* 481–488.

Vandenberg, B. (1981). Environmental and cognitive factors in social play. *Journal of Experimental Child Psychology, 31,*169–175.

Vaughn, B. E., & Waters, E. (1981). Attention structure, sociometric status, and dominance: Interrelations, behavioral correlates, and relationships to social competence. *Developmental Psychology, 17,* 275–288.

Voeltz, L. (1980). Children's attitudes toward handicapped peers. *American Journal of Mental Deficiency, 84,* 455–464.

Voeltz, L. (1982). Effects of structured interactions with severely handicapped peers on children's attitudes. *American Journal of Mental Deficiency, 86,* 380–390.

Warren, D. H. (1977). *Blindness and early childhood development.* New York: American Foundation for the Blind.

Warren, D. H. (1984). *Blindness and early childhood development* (2nd ed., rev.). New York: American Foundation for the Blind.

Whiting, J. W. (1954). In J. M. Tanner & B. Inhelder (Eds.), *Discussions on child development II.* New York: International Universities Press.

Wilson, E. L. (1967). A developmental approach to psychological factors which may inhibit mobility in the visually handicapped person. *New Outlook for the Blind, 61,* 283–289.

Winzer, M., Rogow, S., & David, C. (1987). *Exceptional children in Canada.* Scarborough, Ontario, Canada: Prentice-Hall.

Witkin, H. A., Birhbaum, J., Lomonaco, S., Lehr, S., & Herman, J.

(1938). Cognitive patterning in congenitally totally blind children. *Child Development, 39.*

Workman, S. H. (1986). Teachers' verbalizations and the social interaction of blind preschoolers. *Journal of Visual Impairment & Blindness, 80,* 532–534.

Yarnall, G. D. (1979). Developing eye contact in a visually impaired deaf child. *Education of the Visually Handicapped, 11,* 56–59.

Youniss, J., & Volpe, J. (1978). A relational analysis of children's friendship. In W. Damon (Ed.), *New directions for child development: Vol. 1. Social Cognition* (pp. 1–22). San Francisco: Jossey-Bass.

Zweibelson, I., & Barg, C. F. (1967). Concept development in blind children. *New Outlook for the Blind, 61,* 18–222.

Suggested Readings

BOOKS

Asher, S. R., & Gottman, J. M. (1981). *The development of children's friendships.* London: Cambridge University Press.

Corsaro, W. A. (1985). *Friendship and peer culture in the early years.* Norwood, NJ: Ablex.

Ellis, E., & Whitington, D. (1983). *New directions in social skill training.* London: Croom Helm.

Field, T., Roopnarine, J. L., & Segal, M. (1984). *Friendships in normal and handicapped children.* Norwood, NJ: Ablex.

Gaylord-Ross, R. J. (1989). *Integration strategies for students with handicaps.* Baltimore: Paul H. Brookes.

Kelly, J. A. (1982). *Social skills training: A practical guide for interventions.* New York: Springer.

Rubin, Z. (1980). *Children's friendships.* Cambridge, MA: Harvard University Press.

Sacks, S., & Reardon, M. P. (1989). Maximizing social interaction for students with visual handicaps. In R. Gaylord-Ross (Ed.), *Integration strategies for students with handicaps* (pp. 77–104). Baltimore: Paul H. Brookes.

Strain, P. S., Guralnick, M. J., & Walker, H. M. (1986). *Children's social behavior.* New York: Academic Press.

Swallow, R. M., & Huebner, K. M. (1987). *How to thrive, not just survive: A guide to developing independent life skills for visually impaired children and youths.* New York: American Foundation for the Blind.

Van Hasselt, V. B. (1983). Visual impairment. In M. Hersen, V. B. Van Hasselt, & L. Matson (Eds.), *Behavior therapy for the developmentally and physically disabled* (pp. 109–129). New York: Academic Press.

JOURNAL ARTICLES

Bishop, V. E. (1986). Identifying the components of successful mainstreaming. *Journal of Visual Impairment & Blindness, 80,* 939–946.

Erin, J. N. (1986). Frequencies and types of questions in the language of visually impaired children. *Journal of Visual Impairment & Blindness, 80,* 670–674.

Foster, S. L., & Ritchey, W. L. (1979). Issues in the assessment of social competence in children. *Journal of Applied Behavior Analysis, 12,* 625–638.

Hatch, J. A. (1987). Peer interaction and the development of social competence. *Child Study Journal, 17,* 169–183.

Hatlen, P. H., & Curry, S. A. (1987). In support of specialized programs for blind and visually impaired children: The impact of visual loss on learning. *Journal of Visual Impairment & Blindness, 81,* 7–13.

Hoben, M., & Lindstrom, V. (1980). Evidence of isolation in the mainstream. *Journal of Visual Impairment & Blindness, 74,* 289–292.

Hubbard, C. L. (1983). Reverse mainstreaming sighted children into a visually impaired special day class. *Journal of Visual Impairment & Blindness, 77,* 193–195.

Kekelis, L. S., & Andersen, E. S. (1984). Family communication styles and language development. *Journal of Visual Impairment & Blindness, 78,* 54–65.

Naughton, F., & Sacks, S. Z. (1977). *Hey! What's cooking? A kitchen curriculum for parents of visually handicapped children.* Flosmoor, IL: South Metropolitan Association for Low Incidence Handicapped Children.

Park, H. S., & Gaylord-Ross, R. J. (1989). A problem-solving approach to social skills training in employment settings with mentally retarded youth. *Journal of Applied Behavior Analysis, 22,* 373–380.

Putallaz, M., & Gottman, J. M. (1981). An interactional model of children's entry into peer groups. *Child Development, 52,* 986–994.

Read, L. F. (1989). An examination of the social skills of blind kindergarten children. *Education of the Visually Handicapped, 20*(4), 142-155.

Sacks, S. Z., & Gaylord-Ross, R. J. (1989). Peer-mediated and teacher-directed social skills training for visually impaired students. *Behavior Therapy, 20,* 619–638.

Sisson, L. A., Van Hasselt, V. B., Hersen, M., & Strain, P. (1985). Increasing social behavior in multihandicapped children through peer interaction. *Behavior Modification, 9,* 293–321.

Van Hasselt, V. B., Hersen, M., Kazdin, A. E., Simon, J. A., & Mastanuono, A. K. (1983). Social skills training for blind adolescents. *Journal of Visual Impairment & Blindness, 77,* 99–103.

CURRICULA

Ball, G. (1974). *Magic circle: An overview of the human development program.* La Mesa, CA: Human Development Training Institute.

Camp, B. W., & Bash, M. A. (1985). *Think aloud.* Champaign, IL: Research Press.

Dinkmeyer, D. (1970). *Developing an understanding of self and others (DUSO).* Circle Pines, MN: American Guidance Service.

Goldstein, A. P., Sprafkin, R. P., Gershaw, N. J., & Klein, P. (1980). *Skillstreaming the adolescent.* Champaign, IL: Research Press.

Hazel, J. S., Schumaker, J. B., Sherman, J. A., & Shelden-Wildgen, J. (1982). *ASSET: A social skills program for adolescents.* Champaign, IL: Research Press.

Jackson, N. F., Jackson, D. A., & Monroe, C. (1983). *Getting along with others: Teaching social effectiveness to children.* Champaign, IL: Research Press.

McGinis, E., Goldstein, A. P., Sprafkin, R. P., & Gershaw, J. (1984). *Skillstreaming the elementary school child.* Champaign, IL: Research Press.

Stephens, T. M. (1978). *Social skills in the classroom.* Columbus, OH: Cedars Press.

Walker, H. M., McConnell, S., Holmes, D., Todis, B., Walker, J., & Golden, H. (1983). *The Walker social skills curriculum: The ACCEPTS program.* Austin, TX: Pro Ed.

Walker, H. M., Todis, B., Holmes, D., & Horton, G. (1988). *The Walker social skills curriculum: The ACCESS program.* Austin, TX: Pro Ed.

About the Authors

Robert J. Gaylord-Ross, prior to his recent death, was professor of Special Education, Vanderbilt University, and former professor and coordinator, the Vocational Special Education Program, San Francisco State University. The co-author of *Strategies for Educating Students with Severe Handicaps, Vocational Education for Persons with Handicaps, Integration Strategies for Students with Severe Handicaps,* and *Issues and Research in Special Education, Volume I,* he was also the author of numerous articles on social-skills training, behavioral treatment, and vocational education.

Linda S. Kekelis is a doctoral candidate in special education, the University of California, Berkeley, and San Francisco State University. She has published a wide variety of material relating to early language development and social development of visually impaired children.

P. Ann MacCuspie is coordinator of provincial services, the Atlantic Provinces Special Education Authority, Nova Scotia, Canada. She has worked as an itinerant teacher for visually impaired students, as a classroom teacher at Halifax School for the Blind, and as a provincial consultant in special education.

Janet Macks is an orientation and mobility instructor, Marin County Office of Education, Marin County, California; at the time of writing, she was a research assistant and graduate student in special education, San Francisco State University.

Rona L. Pogrund is a private consultant in visual impairment in Austin, Texas. At the time of writing, she was associate professor, Division of Special Education, Orientation and Mobility Training Program, California State University, Los Angeles.

213

Maureen P. Reardon is an attorney specializing in family law; at the time of writing, she was a teacher of visually impaired students, San Mateo County Office of Education, San Mateo County, California.

Sharon Zell Sacks is associate professor, Division of Special Education and Rehabilitative Services, San Jose State University and San Francisco State University, California. She is the project director for two personnel preparation training grants, the principal investigator for the Social Skills Implementation Project, and the author of numerous publications and presentations concerning the social development of visually impaired children and transition and employment issues. She has worked as a teacher of visually impaired and multiply disabled students in Illinois and California.

Felice A. Strauss is a special education facilitator, Long Beach Unified School District, Long Beach, California; at the time of writing, she was a teacher of visually impaired students in the same district.